THE
THEORY
OF
KNOWLEDGE

—m—

THE
THEORY
OF
KNOWLEDGE

A Thematic Introduction

—⚶—

Paul K. Moser
Dwayne H. Mulder
J.D. Trout

New York   Oxford
OXFORD UNIVERSITY PRESS
1998

Oxford University Press

Oxford New York
Athens   Auckland   Bangkok   Bogota   Bombay   Buenos Aires
Calcutta   Cape Town   Dar es Salaam   Delhi   Florence   Hong Kong
Istanbul   Karachi   Kuala Lumpur   Madras   Madrid   Melbourne
Mexico City   Nairobi   Paris   Singapore   Taipei   Tokyo   Toronto   Warsaw

and associated companies in
Berlin Ibadan

Published by Oxford University Press, Inc.
198 Madison Avenue, New York, New York 10016

Oxford is a registered trademark of Oxford University Press

Library of Congress Cataloging-in-Publication Data
Moser, Paul K., 1957–
The theory of knowledge: a thematic introduction / Paul K. Moser,
Dwayne H. Mulder, J.D. Trout.
p.   cm.
Includes bibliographical references and index.
ISBN 0–19–509465–4 (cloth: alk. paper) —
ISBN 0–19–509466–2 (pbk.: alk. paper)
1. Knowledge, Theory of.   I. Mulder, Dwayne.   II. Trout, J.D.
III. Title.
BD161.M8485 1997   96-52985
121—dc21   CIP

1 3 5 7 9 8 6 4 2

Printed in the United States of America
on acid-free paper

Contents

—◠m◠—

Preface

This book offers a thematic introduction to the theory of knowledge, or epistemology. The book is decidedly not an historical introduction to the field, even though it makes frequent reference to historical figures in epistemology. Instead, it concentrates on substantive developments in the twentieth century, treating the most prominent representative themes in contemporary theory of knowledge.

Quite naturally, philosophers are often swept up in the detailed disputes and subtle arguments of their fields. In this respect, at least, epistemologists follow suit. Many introductory books thus begin with the best of intentions, but nonetheless end up incomprehensible to students altogether new to the field. We have tried to resist the philosophical temptation to inessential detail and subtlety with what has amounted at times to Spartan self-denial. If a few unstinting specialists lack appreciation for an introductory treatment, perhaps their students' responses will compensate.

This book is uniformly a joint effort, even though written by three philosophers with different epistemologies and different emphases in teaching epistemology. No page has escaped review by each of the authors. Our philosophical diversity was actually a distinct advantage. The range of issues on which we agreed has allowed us to advance only general themes and positions in the book, thereby yielding a perspective on epistemology that most instructors and students will find accessible and untendentious.

While genuinely introductory, this book does not pretend to be perfectly neutral on all matters. (We're not even sure that an epistemology text *could* be neutral on every matter.) The book contains not only a thematic treatment of the field that reflects our common judgment about what issues are especially important, but also two modest, but nonetheless positive, unifying positions. The first is a commitment to truth as some kind of correspondence, no matter what one's theory of justification. We thus challenge relativism about truth. The second unifying position is the central role we assign to explanation — a position sometimes called explanationism — in the assessment of justification, both philosophical and scientific. We motivate our explanationism in connection with the longstanding problem of the relation between intuitions and theory in epistemology.

An overarching lesson of this book is that epistemology is alive and well, fortified by recent interaction with the cognitive sciences, decision theory, and cross-cultural studies. Epistemology, we have no doubt, will continue to flourish. We thank the editorial staff at Oxford University Press for excellent assistance.

May 1997   P. K. M.
Chicago, IL   D. H. M.
                                               J. D. T.

THE
THEORY
OF
KNOWLEDGE

1

Epistemology: A First Look

This book introduces the philosophical study of knowledge. It examines the following topics, among others: what knowledge consists in, how we acquire knowledge, how we distinguish knowledge from "mere opinion," how we rely on other people for knowledge, and how skepticism challenges familiar assumptions about knowledge. Why, however, is there a philosophical study of knowledge in the first place? *Perhaps* it would be better to pursue investigations that increase our knowledge of the subjective and objective world rather than worrying about what knowledge itself is. What point, in any case, is there to the philosophical study of knowledge? Why might one be interested in the defining conditions of knowledge, the sources of knowledge, or the limits of knowledge?

Life being all too short, nobody wants to waste valuable time with interminable debates on insignificant topics. Because we are giving our time and energy to the theory of knowledge, we should explain the value of this traditional branch of philosophy. This chapter and the next pursue this task.

WHY STUDY KNOWLEDGE?

People commonly emphasize the importance of having knowledge or at least the resulting power. Accordingly, we aim throughout our lives to acquire knowledge. Sometimes we pursue knowledge simply because we love to learn. Sometimes there are external pressures on us to acquire knowledge, and we might even feel at times like receptacles into which others are continually dumping information. We might be expected to know the Pythagorean theorem, what a dangling modifier is, various facts of world history, the kinetic theory of heat and the atomic theory of matter, and so on.

Much knowledge is handed down to us in school, at work, and at home. We believe, and perhaps even know, many things on the basis of authority. We have, however, acquired some knowledge on our own, independently of the testimony of others. We can know from our own experience, for example, the best way to get home from work, and many people know from their personal experience what it feels like to have a headache. Whether knowledge is picked up from someone else or acquired more directly, we recognize value in *possessing* knowledge: including its value for passing tests, its value in finding our way home, its value in the interest it holds for us, and its value simply in itself.

Because we value knowledge, we can and often should take a critical approach to acquiring knowledge. We should take as much responsibility for our beliefs as is reasonable and, in keeping with this, carefully assess the testimony of others whenever possible. Except in cases of arcane information, we often try to take beliefs accepted initially on hearsay and support them with beliefs accepted on the basis of our own evidence and reasoning.

When receiving information from someone else, we often ask, "Is this person really in a position to *know* what is being reported?" Most of us have, of course, been able to detect some errors in our education. For instance, we sometimes still hear the false claim, even from teachers, that before Columbus everyone thought the earth was flat. Much of what we hear from authoritative sources is arguably correct. The occasional acknowledged error, however, naturally prompts the question of how we can know whether information from the testimony of others is correct. Such error leads us also to ask how we determine for ourselves what testimony to accept and what to reject. The latter question has no easy answer.

Our questioning of sources of information reveals a need for clarification of the defining conditions of knowledge. To ask whether some people really *know* what they report, we need to know what in general is required to know something rather than merely to believe that we know it. Philosophers typically look at the nature of knowledge *generally*, asking what is required for a person genuinely to know that something is true rather than false. A theory of knowledge aims to illuminate such general issues about knowledge.

The value of a philosophical study of knowledge derives in part from the value of possessing knowledge. It's valuable, in many ways, to have knowledge of various sorts, and it's bad to be mistaken about important matters. Consequently, we try to get genuine knowledge and to avoid believing false reports, at least for matters that have some significance, such as health and happiness. So, each of us faces the task of sorting through the barrage of information confronting us every day, in order to accept what's true while rejecting what's false. In this respect, intellectual and practical life is remarkably complex.

Given the importance of gathering correct information and avoiding false beliefs, we need some guidelines for distinguishing true from false beliefs. Philosophers who study knowledge try to identify such guidelines and formulate them generally. One elementary guideline might state that our reliance on a particular source of information should vary inversely with the number of times we have found it mistaken. The more mistakes we find in a certain newspaper, for example, the less we should trust each new report in that paper. Our primary objective is to find (important) truth without falling into error. To pursue truth judiciously, however, we need principles indicating when we ought to accept something as true.

Philosophers call the theory of knowledge "epistemology"— from the ancient Greek terms "episteme" (for knowledge) and "logos" (for theory or explanation). Characterized broadly, epistemology is the philosophical study of the nature, sources, and limits of knowledge. The adjective "epistemological" applies to whatever involves such study of knowledge; it means "having to do with the theory of knowledge." A closely related adjective is "epistemic"; it means "having to do with knowledge." Knowledge, of course, is not the same as a *theory of* knowledge, just as a mind is not the same as a theory of the mind, a psychology.

Philosophical reflection on the conditions and sources of knowledge goes back at least to the ancient Greek philosophers Plato (c. 427–c. 347 B.C.) and Aristotle (384–322 B.C.). Plato's *Theaetetus* and Aristotle's *Posterior Analytics,* more than any other writings, set the stage for epistemology by delimiting the concept and the structure of human knowledge. In the *Theaetetus,* for example, we find Socrates, the central figure in Plato's writings, discussing with some friends how certain reputable teachers know the things that distinguish them as experts. They ask what it is in general that distinguishes those, like teachers, who genuinely know from others who do not know but are in the process of learning. These ancient works still influence, directly and indirectly, much philosophical inquiry about human knowledge.

Epistemology is not unique to the Western philosophical tradition. Indian (Hindu) philosophy, for example, deals extensively with questions in epistemology and logic similar to many of the topics in classical and contemporary European and American philosophy. Indian philosophers have given considerable attention to problems of gathering and assessing evidence, problems of perceptual knowledge, and the role of reasoning in knowledge, among many others. Fundamental questions regarding the nature of knowledge are likely to arise in any culture. After all, everyone has some stake in distinguishing truth from error, wisdom from ignorance, and the path to knowledge from the path to ignorance.

Different cultures might handle philosophical questions about knowledge differently. Some cultures, for example, might emphasize the social nature of knowledge, stressing the place of scientific or religious authorities, scholars, political and military leaders, or other acquaintances as sources of knowledge. Other cultures might focus on the individual as a solitary figure sifting through incoming evidence (whether from the testimony of others or from more direct experience) and deciding what to accept or reject. Some critics of Western philosophical traditions have charged them with excessive emphasis on the individual as a solitary knower. This charge has led recently to increasing attention to the social aspects of knowledge, a topic discussed in Chapter 6. If there has been an imbalance here in the history of Western epistemology, it is likely to be corrected to some extent in contemporary epistemology, owing to its contributions from many different cultural and intellectual backgrounds. Recent epistemology has also received important contributions from feminist philosophers. In what follows, we shall return to such developments in recent epistemology.

SOME DOUBTS ABOUT KNOWLEDGE

Epistemologists have discussed, in addition to the defining conditions and the sources of knowledge, the *extent* of human knowledge. They have asked how far human knowledge can extend. Two extreme positions would be:

1. Humans can know, at least in principle, every truth about reality.
2. Humans can (or at least do) know nothing.

Many philosophers develop some position in between these two extremes. In particular, many philosophers would reject *1* on the ground that human beings are *finite* knowers. There seem to be limits to how much we can know. Just as there are many things a dog, for example, cannot know or understand, so also there are probably many things beyond the cognitive grasp of humans. Evolutionary theory and some major religions agree in their supporting the thesis of human cognitive limitations, on the ground that humans are finite creatures — even if they divide over the explanation of this finitude.

Most, but not all, philosophers reject the previous skeptical view 2. Many philosophers find it obvious that we know at least *some* things, if only things about personal experiences or household physical objects. Others have claimed, however, that we really have no knowledge. Such philosophers admit that people typically feel confident that they have some knowledge, but these philosophers insist that our apparent cases of knowledge are mere illusions. The stronger skeptical claim that humans *cannot* (and not just *do not*) have knowledge at all typically derives from a belief that the *conditions* for knowledge are extremely demanding, so demanding that we cannot meet them.

Some people may naturally think that the conditions for knowledge are very demanding. This is especially the case if people want to emphasize the distinction between "genuine" knowledge (say, scientific knowledge about how the world really is, which may seem rare) and mere opinion (say, mere opinion about the effectiveness of new diet plans, which may seem widespread), or if they reflect much on the vulnerability of many of our most confident claims to knowledge. It is disturbing, in any case, to observe how someone's most firmly held beliefs can simply turn out to be wrong.

Consider a person living a couple of centuries ago who entertains the possibility of communicating almost instantaneously with a friend a thousand miles away. An eighteenth-century gentleman would probably insist that he *knows*, just as surely as he knows anything in the world, that such long-distance communication is impossible. Of course, we *know* that he's wrong. He does *not* know that such communication is impossible, because we all have communicated in just this way many times. What is commonplace knowledge to us was, in this case, incomprehensible to our ancestors. They made confident claims to *know* some of the things we now know to be wrong. They had the highest degree of confidence, but still failed to have genuine knowledge. Some people may be tempted to conclude from such cases that the conditions for genuine knowledge must be very demanding.

Some philosophers, having reflected on the previous considerations, conclude that the conditions for knowledge are very demanding indeed. René Descartes (1596–1650), for example, entertained that much of what he had learned from his formal education, and had accepted as established knowledge, turned out after careful examination to be false. He ended up requiring something akin to what we call *certainty* as a condition for philosophical knowledge: in particular, certainty as *indubitability*, the absence of *possible* doubt about correctness. Another kind of certainty requires *infallibility*, the absence of any real *possibility* of error. It seems that very few, if any, propositions enjoy the kind of certainty sought by some philosophers. Such seemingly invulnerable propositions as "I think" and "I doubt" are, unfortunately, few and far between.

Our eighteenth-century gentleman, if he thought about the matter carefully, would have to admit that he is not *certain* that instantaneous long-distance communication is impossible. He has no definite notion of how it would be possible, but he would probably have to admit the abstract possibility of such communication. *Perhaps* this fact indicates that he did not really *know* that it's impossible to talk instantaneously to his distant friend. He did not meet the condition of certainty and therefore did not really have knowledge, *if* knowledge requires certainty.

Most contemporary epistemologists have rejected the demand for certainty as a prerequisite of knowledge. We can know things without being certain about them, that is, without their being either indubitable or infallible. Our eighteenth-century gentleman knew and we know, for instance, that lightning does not occur in a completely clear, cloudless sky. We know this, even though we admit that it is neither indubitable nor infallible. We know this, even though we are not certain of it. So, certainty does not seem to be a prerequisite for knowledge.

We shall examine the defining conditions of knowledge in later chapters. For now, we note that a very demanding condition on knowledge, such as the requirement of certainty, can lead to the skeptical view that we never actually acquire knowledge. Setting the prerequisites of knowledge very high can lead to the view that we have no knowledge. This would amount to what some have called a low skeptical victory by high redefinition of knowledge.

The philosophical position that people cannot or at least do not have knowledge is *skepticism*. This term is familiar from various nonphilosophical contexts.

A recent newspaper headline read, "China says it will agree to nuclear test ban treaty; U.S. skeptical" (*Chicago Tribune*, June 7, 1996). In this case, the term "skeptical" means that the United States is *doubtful* that China will adhere to the nuclear test ban treaty. In philosophy, a skeptic does not merely have *some* doubt that people have knowledge. The thoroughgoing skeptic asserts that people have no knowledge at all. Of course, if the skeptic claimed to *know* that no one has any knowledge, the skeptic would risk self-contradiction. It would be a careless skeptic indeed who claimed to *know*, for example, that knowledge requires certainty, to *know* that we never have complete certainty, and therefore to *know* that we never have knowledge. Skeptics must, in any case, be careful in presenting their skepticism, lest the previous kind of self-contradiction threaten.

Traditionally, skepticism has been an important source of motivation for epistemologists. Many philosophers throughout the history of Western epistemology have tried to refute the skeptic by showing that we actually possess some knowledge. They have tried to show that we possess genuine knowledge by clarifying the defining conditions and main sources of human knowledge and by demonstrating that we at least *can* satisfy the conditions of knowledge with the cognitive resources available to us. The topic of skepticism will recur in various discussions throughout this book, particularly in Chapter 8.

Skepticism comes in various forms. *Total* skepticism denies the existence of *any* human knowledge. *Partial* skepticism denies the existence of only some particular type or types of knowledge. Some philosophers, for example, deny knowledge that God exists, without denying other types of knowledge, such as knowledge that household physical objects exist. Others deny theoretical scientific knowledge, such as knowledge of the structure of the atom, while defending claims to knowledge of our own thoughts and feelings. Partial skeptics claim to find some defect in a particular type of knowledge rather than in knowledge generally. To understand such claims, we must understand some distinctions between various types of knowledge, such as scientific knowledge and mathematical knowledge. We shall soon return to such distinctions.

Skepticism has its historical roots in ancient Greek philosophy. One type of skepticism goes back to Socrates (469–399 B.C.); another type stems from Pyrrho of Elis (c. 365–c.270 B.C.). Socratic skepticism is called "Academic skepticism," because it flourished in Plato's Academy after Plato's death. Socrates was told by the Oracle at Delphi (roughly, the local fortune-teller) that he was the wisest of all men because he knew that he had no knowledge, whereas all other men fancied themselves quite knowledgeable about things they did not really know. Academic skeptics develop this point into a philosophical doctrine: The only thing a person can know is that he or she really knows nothing other than this doctrine. This is a strong denial of the existence of human knowledge, other than the knowledge that we really know nothing else.

Pyrrhonian skepticism, in contrast, makes no bold (or, some might say, dogmatic) claim like that of Academic skeptics. Pyrrhonian skepticism emphasizes suspension of judgment on most matters. Instead of engaging in the seemingly unending intellectual wrangling of the philosophers, Pyrrhonians recommend that we should try to find a balance of argument both for and against any position and hence refrain from accepting any conclusion. Pyrrhonians claim that our recognizing suspension of judgment as the only rational action leads us to a state of calm, or quietude, free from heated debates over controversial theses. This quietude constitutes an improved quality of life, if not also a sense of enlightenment, according to Pyrrhonians.

Most epistemologists, we have noted, do not go to the extreme of total skepticism. Many epistemologists aim not to set knowledge beyond our reach or to escape the quest for knowledge but rather to make many of our ordinary claims to knowledge more secure by *explaining* knowledge. They seek to explain what knowledge consists in and how we get it. An epistemologist might be greatly impressed, for example, with the power of science for expanding our knowledge of the world, and thus seek an explanation of how science advances knowledge.

Although many epistemologists oppose total skepticism, we should not simply dismiss skeptical challenges, even if we believe that we do have a substantial amount of knowledge. Some skeptical challenges to knowledge are instructive, because they raise difficulties at least for our initial, naive explanations of how knowledge arises. A problem confronts, for example, our eighteenth-century gentleman who was quite confident in his belief but turned out not to have genuine knowledge.

One option, noted previously, is to become pessimistic about the prospects for knowledge of any kind. There are other options too, options that maintain optimism about acquiring knowledge while acknowledging the fallibility (susceptibility to error) of our eighteenth-century gentleman and likewise of ourselves. Epistemologists assess such options in detail. In this connection, skeptics motivate us to clarify what is required of a more sophisticated explanation of human knowledge. Without skeptical challenges, we might become complacent about understanding ourselves as knowledge-acquiring agents. Skeptics raise some hard questions, and they have led philosophers to make significant revisions in their thinking about acceptable methods of knowledge acquisition. We shall see later, in Chapter 8, how skeptical concerns about circularity in justification raise a serious, if not fatal, problem for optimism about establishing claims to know.

Skeptical questions about truth and evidence have a second benefit. They promote a healthy measure of epistemic humility. It is tempting, for philosophers as well as for nonphilosophers, to claim certainty in things that are really not certain. Many people fail, in other words, to recognize the magnitude of our fallibility as knowers. They are thus unwilling to admit doubt and possible error about things that are open to doubt and error. Unwillingness to admit the possibility of being wrong when one really could be wrong on some issue is *dogmatism*. A person who refuses to admit the possibility of being wrong in some belief, if that belief really might be wrong, has a dogmatic attitude toward that belief or a dogmatic acceptance of that belief. Many skeptics try to eliminate dogmatism, and this is usually an appropriate aim, given human fallibility. Most epistemologists, as suggested, steer a course between excessive minimization of our abilities as knowers, on the one hand, and excessive minimization of our shortcomings as knowers, on the other hand. Skeptics helpfully keep us away from the latter course, although they might steer us too near the former course.

Some people seem to entertain skeptical worries based on their acceptance of *relativism* concerning truth. The connection between skepticism and relativism requires clarification. A relativist concerning truth asserts that the truth of a claim can hold only relative to some knower (that is, someone who either accepts or rejects that claim) or perhaps to some group of knowers. The relativist about truth denies that there is *absolute* truth (that is, truth that does not vary from person to person or from group to group), at least with respect to some matters. Theological topics offer familiar examples, as some people claim that the statement "God exists" is true for those who believe but false for those who do not believe. This, whether true or false, is a relativist claim. Some people might favor this position as a way to avoid sensitive confrontations between believers and nonbelievers, but we need not explain here why some people become relativists.

The concept of the relativity of truth is perhaps still unclear. An example from a nonepistemic context might clarify things. A good example of an obligation that is relative is the obligation (in some places) to drive on the right-hand side of the road. *Relative* to American laws, for instance, one has an obligation to drive on the right-hand side. *Relative* to English laws, however, one has an obligation to drive on the left-hand side. The obligation to drive one way or the other exists, in this example, only relative to a legal code, and legal codes can vary from place to place. The obligation is merely relative, because beyond the respective legal systems, there is no objective, or absolute, obligation to drive one way or the other.

Many people would claim, by contrast, that the obligation not to torture babies, for example, is not relative. This obligation might exist relative to some legal code prohibiting mistreatment of babies, but it arguably has an objective existence beyond any such legal code as well. Many people, in any case, regard it as an objective obligation, binding irrespective of legal codes. Realists about moral obligations would claim that it is thus objective. Some of our laws seem to codify some pre-existing, objective obligations of this sort, such as the obligation not to murder or to torture. Other laws, however, are obviously relative, being intended to create some obligation. The obligations created by the institution of legal codes exist only relative to those codes. The pre-existing obligations that we try to codify in our laws are arguably nonrelative, or objective. Although it is noncontroversial that some obligations are relative to legal codes, it remains highly controversial whether truth is relative to an individual's or a culture's beliefs.

A relativist about truth might be tempted to be a skeptic about human knowledge, on the ground that knowledge is impossible because truth is merely relative. A relativist might argue, for example, that you can't really *know* that killing babies is wrong, because it is wrong only relative to your culture and might be acceptable in some other cultures. Perhaps more plausibly, one might argue that you can't really know that abortion is wrong (or right) because different people have such fundamentally different attitudes toward it. This line of argument for relativism is called "the argument from disagreement." Relativism about truth does not, however, really lead to skepticism. Relativism about truth leads in the opposite direction.

If the truth is relative, say, to your own beliefs, then your prospects for acquiring knowledge are much better than if truth is objective and thus difficult to acquire. Relativism makes *truth* very easy to get and, correspondingly, it makes *knowledge* easy to get. A consequence of relativism is that what I know to be true, you might know to be false, because possibly for me it is true and for you it is false. Given relativism, knowledge may thus vary dramatically from person to person (or from culture to culture), yet there will still be knowledge, most likely in abundance. Of course, a relativist about truth could set other standards for knowledge very high (say, with regard to justification), but this would be atypical.

Skepticism flourishes with a view of truth as entirely objective. Some philosophers have emphasized so strongly the distinction between the way things *seem* to us (for example, that the pencil submerged halfway in a glass of water is actually bent) and the way things objectively *are* (the pencil is actually straight) that they despair of our ever being able to know how things objectively are. Some others despair only of our ever being able to *tell whether we know* how things objectively are, admitting that we might actually acquire knowledge and objective truth.

Some philosophers support skepticism only by postulating a significant gap between truth (or, the objective world) and our cognitive powers. One can highlight such a gap either by making truth unattainably mind-independent (or, objective) or by alleging severe limits in our cognitive powers (or both). A skeptic might say that all we ever have to go on, in our quest for objectivity, is our limited experience and that the truth, the objective fact of the matter, always stands beyond that experience. In addition, a skeptic may emphasize a troublesome circularity in all available testing of the reliability of our cognitive sources (for example, perception, memory, introspection), on the ground that we cannot take leave of our cognitive resources to test their reliability (that is, their truth conduciveness) in a noncircular manner. (Chapter 8 will elucidate the latter problem.)

Philosophers commonly distinguish two kinds of skepticism: *knowledge* skepticism and *justification* skepticism. Unrestricted knowledge skepticism asserts that no one knows anything. Unrestricted justification skepticism asserts that no one is ever justified (or, warranted) in believing anything. Knowledge skepticism allows that we are sometimes justified in believing something, but it claims that our justified beliefs never measure up as genuine knowledge, perhaps because knowledge, unlike justification, is immune to threat from the knower's acquiring new evidence. For example, before modern genetics many people may have been justified in believing, on the evidence then available to them, that giraffes have long necks as a result of their stretching for the only

available foliage in trees. Such justified belief came to be undermined by the acquisition of new evidence concerning the internal
genetic mechanisms of the heritability of giraffe traits. Knowledge,
in contrast, is immune to such undermining, or defeat, by new evidence. Justification skepticism denies that we have, or even that
we ever can have, legitimate grounds for any belief. We shall
return to the topic of skepticism in more detail in Chapter 8. For
now, the distinction between knowledge and justified belief
requires some clarification.

Traditional Definition of Knowledge

Epistemology in the Western philosophical tradition has until
recently offered a prominent definition of knowledge that ana-
lyzes knowledge into three essential components: justification,
truth, and belief. According to this analysis, propositional knowledge is, by definition, justified true belief. This definition is called
the *tripartite analysis of knowledge* and *the traditional analysis*. Many
philosophers find inspiration for this view in Plato's *Theaetetus*.
Epistemologists typically focus on *propositional knowledge*: knowledge *that* something is the case, as opposed to knowledge of how
to do something. Consider, for example, the difference between
knowing *that* a bicycle moves by compliance with certain laws of
motion and knowing *how* to ride a bicycle. Obviously, the former
knowledge is not required by the latter.

The content of propositional knowledge can be expressed in a
proposition, that is, what is meant by a declarative sentence. (People using different languages can nonetheless assert the same
proposition: For example, "It is raining" and "Es regnet" mean
the same thing and thus express the same proposition.) Knowledge *how* to do something is, by contrast, a skill or competence in
performing a certain task. We shall not examine such competence
knowledge; it is a topic worthy of a book of its own. The traditional
analysis of propositional knowledge implies that knowledge is a
species of *belief.* If you don't believe that Madagascar is in the
Indian Ocean, you don't know that Madagascar is in the Indian

Ocean. So, as philosophers sometimes say, believing is a *logically necessary condition* for knowing. It would be odd indeed for you to claim to know something but deny believing what you allegedly know. Belief seems required for propositional knowledge.

Belief is not sufficient, or adequate, for knowledge. Many beliefs clearly do not qualify as knowledge, as they are obviously false. Some people still believe, for example, that the earth is flat; there's even a dues-paying society of such people in North America. Even so, they do not *know* that the earth is flat, for the earth, it turns out, is not flat. To know something, to have genuine knowledge, we must be *correct* in what we believe. You don't know what isn't so, that is, what is false. Hence, the second essential condition for knowledge identified in the tripartite analysis is *truth*. Knowledge requires not only belief, but also true belief.

True belief is not itself sufficient for knowledge. Many true beliefs obviously do not qualify as knowledge. If you just spontaneously form the belief that your uncle Hud, who is nowhere in the vicinity, is currently standing up, and this belief just happens to turn out to be true, you still do not thereby know that uncle Hud is currently standing up. The belief lacks *supporting reasons*; it was formed just on a whim and enjoys no suitable backing. The belief turned out to be true coincidentally, relative to your evidence. For a true belief to be knowledge, it must have what philosophers call *justification, warrant,* or *evidence*. (Some philosophers use the latter three terms interchangeably.)

Justification is the third essential condition for knowledge in the tripartite analysis. Justification for a belief must include some good reasons for regarding the belief as true. Philosophers debate what such good reasons amount to, but the claim that a belief needs some kind of support to qualify as knowledge is widely accepted among philosophers. So, the three essential conditions for knowledge are belief, truth, and justification, and these three together are supposed to be sufficient for knowledge. Within the last few decades, philosophers have discovered that these three conditions are not really sufficient for knowledge; something else is required. We shall return to these developments in Chapter 5. According to the traditional tripartite analysis, however, knowledge is justified true belief. If you have good reasons in support of the truth of your belief, and your belief is true and is based on good reasons, then you have knowledge, according to the traditional analysis.

The traditional analysis of knowledge allows for justified false belief. In fact, justified false beliefs appear to be common. At one time, many people were justified in believing that the earth is flat. Their belief was wrong, of course, but given their best available evidence, they had justifying supporting reasons for their belief. Because their belief was mistaken, they did not know that the earth is flat. Our denying them knowledge here is not an indictment of their personal character. We are not criticizing them or faulting them when we deny their claim to knowledge. We rather are pointing out that their belief was mistaken and, in this respect, their evidence was misleading regarding the truth but nonetheless constituted justifying support for them at that time. At times, we are all in a similar situation. Although they satisfied the belief condition and the justification condition for knowledge, they failed to meet the truth condition for knowledge. Justified false belief, we can now see, is not knowledge. (Chapter 9 will return to the topic of justification and relativism.)

All three of the essential conditions for knowledge have attracted vigorous philosophical disputes, and we shall examine some of these disputes in subsequent chapters. Philosophers have rarely disagreed about whether belief is required for knowledge, but they have often disagreed about the nature of belief itself. In addition, many cognitive psychologists have entered the fray with empirical research on the cognitive mechanisms of belief. Chapter 3 will return to this topic. Philosophers generally agree that truth is required for knowledge, but they have offered some opposing ideas about what it is for a belief to be true. Chapter 4 will return to the truth condition for knowledge. Theories of epistemic justification make up one of the most prominent areas of contemporary epistemology. Chapter 5 will return to this topic.

KNOWLEDGE AND EXPERIENCE

One central epistemological debate, involving the sources of knowledge (see Chapter 6), concerns the importance of sense experience in our acquisition of knowledge. Many philosophers agree that we acquire a lot of our knowledge through sense experience. You often acquire knowledge about something by seeing it for yourself, by hearing it for yourself, or by touching, smelling, or tasting it for yourself. You might know, for example, that there is a lilac bush in the immediate vicinity by smelling its fragrance. Is sense experience the only way to gain knowledge? Do we ever know anything independently of sense experience?

Consider your knowledge that the sum of the interior angles of a Euclidean triangle is 180 degrees. This knowledge may be somehow related to sense experience, perhaps in virtue of our having perceptual representations of a triangle. We apparently do not depend on sense experience, however, to know that *all* Euclidean triangles have interior angles equal to 180 degrees. We do not derive this knowledge from an *empirical* survey of many triangles. Rather, it seems to be based only on our *concept* of what a Euclidean triangle is. That is, this knowledge seems to derive only from *reason*, and not from sense experience. So, some knowledge might not depend on sense experience in the way that familiar knowledge of the existence of a nearby lilac bush does.

Epistemologists have special terms for the types of knowledge we have just distinguished. Knowledge depending on experience is called *a posteriori* knowledge. To remember this term, it may help to think of knowledge that comes "posterior to," or "after," sense experience, although the term does not really refer to "before" or "after." Knowledge that does not depend on experience is called *a priori* knowledge. Such knowledge is "prior" to experience in a logical sense, though not necessarily prior to experience in time. The difference between *a priori* and *a posteriori* knowledge is a difference in the function of experience in the justification of known propositions.

We depend on experience to tell us that all stop signs are red in a way that we do not depend on experience to tell us that all stop signs indicate that one must stop. There is nothing in the mere idea of a stop sign that necessitates its being red. Stop signs could have been purple — or any other color, for that matter. To know *firsthand* that all stop signs are red, you would have to look at enough stop signs to convince yourself that they are in fact all red. This, obviously, could be a major project. It is part of the very idea of a stop sign, however, that it indicates that a driver should stop.

Stop signs *by definition* function to tell drivers to stop; it is this function that makes them stop signs. If you found some street sign that did not (or, better, could not) function in this way, you could deduce that it is not a stop sign. You don't need to examine a large number of stop signs, find that they all indicate drivers should stop, and then conclude, on the basis of the pattern found, that *all* stop signs function in this way. In a sense, you know "prior" to any empirical study of stop signs that they function in this way. You know this in a way that you could not have known prior to an empirical study that all stop signs are red.

The claim that all stop signs tell one to stop differs from the claim that all stop signs are red. The former claim is *analytic*, being a definitional truth. It follows from the *definition* of a stop sign that they all somehow indicate that one should stop. A stop sign *just is* a sign that tells one to stop. Analytic truths are true simply in virtue of the meaning of terms, or the analysis of concepts. Another example is the claim that all bachelors are unmarried. Being unmarried is part of the definition of "bachelor." By contrast, the claim that all stop signs are red is a *synthetic* proposition. There is nothing in the mere concept of a sign indicating a stop that requires that the sign be red. We had reasons for making them red, of course. For instance, the color red is good for attracting attention. Still, stop signs *could* have been some other color. The claim that all stop signs are red does not derive just from an analysis of the very concept of a stop sign. Rather, it is a *synthesis* of the concept of a stop sign and the concept of the color red. We are relating these two concepts to each other in a way that is not dictated just by their definitions.

Philosophers debate whether all our *a priori* knowledge is knowledge of analytic propositions. It seems clear that we can know a synthetic proposition *a posteriori*, if our experience appropriately indicates that the synthesis of concepts we are considering is correct. We know by experience, *a posteriori*, that stop signs are red. We can know analytic truths independently of experience, *a priori*. We know *a priori* that all stop signs are signs. Since we can know analytic propositions *a priori*, we don't need *a posteriori* justification for them. You would not (we hope) try to convince someone that all stop signs are signs by driving around town to confirm that they all turn out to be *signs*. Imagine yourself: "Look, there's another stop sign, and look at that — it's a *sign*, just like all the others!" You don't need to do this because a stop sign is by definition a particular type of sign. So we don't try to demonstrate analytic truths *a posteriori*. We can justify some synthetic truths *a posteriori*, and we can demonstrate some analytic truths *a priori*.

The question remains whether any synthetic truth is justified *a priori*. Recent developments in the philosophy of language have complicated treatment of the relation between the analytic–synthetic distinction, on the one hand, and the *a priori–a posteriori* distinction, on the other. (The topic of the following few paragraphs is thus somewhat demanding but important to recent work on the *a priori*.) Some philosophers think that some synthetic truths can be known, and thus justified, *a priori*. Contingently true propositions are possibly false; that is, if the world had been different in certain ways, they would have been false. Many philosophers have assumed that a proposition is knowable *a priori* only if it is necessarily true (that is, not possibly false), on the ground that if a proposition is possibly false, then it requires for its justification supporting evidence from sensory experience. Contingent truths, according to this traditional view, are not candidates for *a priori* knowledge.

Saul Kripke (1980) has recently argued that some contingently true propositions are knowable *a priori*. He offers the example of one's knowledge that stick *S* is 1 meter long at a certain time, where stick *S* is the standard meter-bar in Paris. If we use stick *S* to "fix the reference" of the term "1 meter," then, according to Kripke, we can know *a priori* that stick *S* is 1 meter long. The truth that stick *S* is 1 meter long is contingent rather than necessary, as *S* might not have been 1 meter long. Application of high heat to *S*, for instance, would have changed its length. It seems arguable, then, that some contingent truths are knowable *a priori*, contrary to what many philosophers have assumed. This matter has prompted considerable discussion among contemporary philosophers, with some still contending that no contingently true proposition is knowable *a priori*.

Some philosophers have noted, with regard to Kripke's meter example, that "1 meter" can be used either as (a) the name of the length of *S* whatever that length may be or as (b) the name of a particular length singled out by a speaker. Given option *a*, these philosophers hold, the claim that stick *S* is 1 meter long will be necessary and knowable *a priori*, and given option *b*, the claim that stick *S* is 1 meter long will be contingent and knowable only *a posteriori*. If these philosophers are right, we have to look elsewhere for a synthetic truth knowable *a priori*.

Kripke's meter example offers, according to some contemporary philosophers, a synthetic truth knowable a priori. Immanuel Kant (1724–1804) held that some synthetic truths — for example, those of geometry — have a kind of necessity that cannot be derived from experience, and can be known *a priori*. Such synthetic truths, Kant argued, can be known just on the basis of pure reason and pure understanding, independently of evidence from sensory experience. Kant's doctrine of synthetic *a priori* truths still generates controversy among philosophers, specifically in connection with such apparently synthetic propositions as "Nothing can be green and red all over" and "A straight line is the shortest path between two points." Some philosophers still hold the minority view, in the tradition of Kant, that the truths of epistemology, and of philosophy in general, are necessary synthetic truths knowable *a priori*. (See Pap 1958 for a survey of prominent views about the synthetic *a priori*.)

The distinctions between *a priori* and *a posteriori* knowledge and between analytic and synthetic propositions will prove useful in many of the subsequent discussions. Beyond the question whether there is any source of knowledge independent of sense experience, there are many questions about the workings of sense experience itself and how an experience leads to knowledge. Empirical research in cognitive psychology, brain science, and other fields tells us much about how sense experience works (and sometimes fails to work). A central philosophical question is how sensation leads to perception of our surrounding environment. Many philosophical topics fit under the heading of problems of *perception*. Another important source of knowledge is *memory*, which presents many complications of its own. *Testimony* from other people is also an important source of knowledge, but it obviously cannot be trusted uncritically. Chapter 6 will return to these matters.

INTUITIONS AND THEORY

We now have some of the terms and distinctions enabling us to study the *conditions*, *sources*, and *extent* of human knowledge. A final introductory point about methodology is noteworthy. Many theories in epistemology draw heavily on our ordinary intuitions about the nature of knowledge for their support. We have already been drawing on our intuitions to achieve agreement, for example, that knowledge is a species of *belief* that also requires *truth* and some kind of *justification*. We considered, for instance, the case of someone claiming to *know* that Madagascar is in the Indian Ocean while denying *belief* that Madagascar is in the Indian Ocean. We judge, when thinking about such a case, that it harbors inconsistency. So we come to agree that one must believe something in order to know it. Epistemologists often rely on intuitions, or judgments, of this sort (roughly, intuitions about what is true and what is false) to support their epistemological theories.

We should not be casual in our reliance on our intuitions. Our common-sense intuitions about knowledge might need to be corrected by some more general, theoretical considerations in epistemology. We have to balance considerations of the overall plausibility of our ordinary intuitions against considerations of the overall plausibility of epistemological theories. We need to balance them against each other because intuitions have implications about the acceptability of theories and theories have implications about the acceptability of our intuitions. This might seem perplexing now, but it will be made clear throughout the book.

For now, the main point is that our common-sense intuitions about the nature of knowledge can themselves be adjusted, corrected, or even rejected in light of our acceptance of more general, theoretical claims about the nature of knowledge. For example, common-sense intuitions about the stationary character of the earth are correctable by established astronomical theory. Chapter 9 will return to this topic.

In sum, then, we can see that the theory of knowledge merits careful study for a variety of reasons. For example, skeptical worries of various sorts commonly motivate people to think more critically about the essential conditions, sources, and limits of human knowledge. The traditional definition of knowledge identifies the essential conditions of knowledge as belief, truth, and justification. We shall study each of these components in more detail, and we shall find (in Chapter 5) a need for an additional restriction on the definition of knowledge. We already have some of the basic concepts, such as the concepts of *a priori* and *a posteriori* knowledge, that will allow us to discuss in more detail the conditions, sources, and limits of human knowledge. Throughout our discussions, we shall give special attention to the roles of intuitions and theoretical considerations in epistemology. We turn now to explaining human propositional knowledge.

2

Explaining Knowledge

Some people, we need not be reminded, think they know a lot more than they actually know. Perhaps this is true even of most of us at times, although we see no reason to name names in public. Clearly, if at times unfortunately, our believing that our preferred answer to a test question is correct does not automatically make our answer correct. Likewise, our thinking that we know something does not mean that we actually know it.

A theory of knowledge should, at a minimum, clarify the difference between genuine knowledge and merely apparent knowledge, between the real thing and likely counterfeits. In failing to clarify this difference, a theory of knowledge will be defective in one of its central tasks: to elucidate what genuine knowledge consists in. Inasmuch as knowledge is a valuable commodity for us (for instance, in knowing the best means to our goals, whatever our goals), a theory of knowledge should enable us to separate counterfeits from the real article. Counterfeits, at least in many cases, will ultimately disappoint. Consider, for example, the drastic consequences of the lack of genuine knowledge concerning the reliability of the infamous O-rings on the space shuttle. Given that knowledge is valuable, we should aim to acquire it and to acquire reasonable means for acquiring it. A theory of knowledge promises to enhance our means for acquiring knowledge. This chapter examines some main goals of a theory of knowledge.

THE SCOPE OF EPISTEMOLOGY

Ideally, an epistemology would elucidate all potential domains of knowledge, including scientific knowledge, mathematical knowledge, ordinary perceptual knowledge, ethical knowledge, and religious knowledge. In this respect, an ideal epistemology would be comprehensive, maximally explanatory. We note this ideal even though its realization evades us. The ideal at least identifies a goal worthy of serious pursuit, given that knowledge in the various domains is valuable.

As suggested in Chapter 1, a *skeptic* about a certain domain of knowledge denies, usually on the basis of argument and at the risk of being disturbing, that humans actually have that kind of knowledge. Our talk of *potential* domains of knowledge avoids begging questions against skeptics about the reality of certain kinds of knowledge. An epistemology can elucidate a *concept* (or, what is the same, a *notion* or an *idea*) of scientific knowledge, for instance, without committing the epistemologist to the actual existence of scientific knowledge. Analogously, your clarifying the *concept* of a unicorn does not require your believing that unicorns actually exist. Even most philosophers can concur at this point — a rare achievement among those thriving on disagreement. Concepts do not owe their meaningfulness to their having actual instances; otherwise, we could not think about fictional objects, and much classic literature would suffer accordingly. Intelligible notions of unicorns and trolls flourish, for better or worse, without an actual population of unicorns and trolls.

While distinguishing various potential domains of knowledge, some philosophers disagree about which potential domains of knowledge qualify as actual cases of knowledge rather than as tales. Disagreement thus runs deep in the theory of knowledge (in keeping with philosophy generally), but disagreement, we shall see, is no reason for despair or even relativism about truth. Persistent disagreement makes trouble for *consensus* but not for truth independent of opinion. We should not, of course, conflate truth and consensus, regardless of some opposing tendencies in the mass media. At one time people vigorously *disagreed* over whether our planet revolves around the sun, but it was nonetheless *true* that the earth revolves around the sun. The move toward human agreement in this area did not change the nature of celestial motion.

The aforementioned potential domains of knowledge have something noteworthy in common: They are all potential domains of *knowledge*. That is, they are specific instances of the general category *knowledge*. This may seem obvious, but it comes as disputable news to some philosophers, for whom most news is likewise subject to dispute. In elucidating the general category of knowledge, an epistemology will explain what unites the various potential domains of knowledge. This task is fundamental to explaining any of the potential domains of knowledge; for if we do not understand the general category of knowledge, we shall not comprehend talk of scientific knowledge, mathematical knowledge, ordinary perceptual knowledge, ethical knowledge, or religious knowledge. Note this analogy: If we do not understand the category of *snark* (for which Lewis Carroll is rightly lauded), we shall fail likewise to comprehend talk of *scientific* snark, *mathematical* snark, *ethical* snark, and so on. A comprehensive epistemology will thus elucidate the general category of knowledge as a prerequisite for clarifying specific potential domains of knowledge.

The scope, or breadth, of an epistemology is determined by the range of potential domains of knowledge it explains. An epistemology with a narrow scope might elucidate the category of ordinary perceptual knowledge, for example, but make no contribution to the understanding of any other potential domain of knowledge. Given the notable complexities within any individual potential domain of knowledge (and they are indeed notable), many contemporary epistemologists settle for elucidating one domain of knowledge. Still, even a narrow epistemology should clarify the general category of knowledge it presupposes, as talk of a particular kind of knowledge will be obscure to the extent that the underlying general notion of knowledge is unclear. If the notion of knowledge is obscure, the notion of scientific knowledge, for instance, will be correspondingly unclear. At least, prephilosophical wisdom counsels thus.

THE CONCEPT OF KNOWLEDGE

Some philosophers, influenced by either the "ordinary-language" philosophical view that all concepts are "open textured" or Ludwig Wittgenstein's already classic *Philosophical Investigations* (1958), have denied that a single general notion of knowledge underlies the various potential domains of knowledge. They hold that various uses of a general term, such as "knowledge" or "game," need not have a common general meaning, but may be related only by diverse similarities (so-called "family resemblances") not shared by all the uses in question. According to this view, the standard use of "knowledge" in "mathematical knowledge," for example, may mean something different from the standard use of "knowledge" in "religious knowledge." Indeed, some proponents of Wittgenstein's view of meaning hold that these uses do differ in meaning. They would thus recommend that we abandon the traditional philosophical effort to characterize human knowledge *in general*, on the ground that there is no meaningful notion of human knowledge in general.

How should we assess disputes about what the term "knowledge" means? One natural strategy would be to ask people what they mean by "knowledge" in various contexts, on the assumption that most people know what they themselves mean by "knowledge." Some philosophers hold that many people use "knowledge" univocally, with a single meaning, in standard talk of scientific knowledge, mathematical knowledge, ordinary perceptual knowledge, ethical knowledge, philosophical knowledge, and religious knowledge. If these philosophers are right, many people use a single general notion of knowledge as a common core in the aforementioned potential domains of knowledge. It does not follow, however, that *everyone* does so. Other people, in keeping with Wittgenstein's position, may use "knowledge" equivocally, with various meanings, in talk of the various potential domains of knowledge. If so, different groups of people use "knowledge" with different senses. Such variation in linguistic meaning is a real possibility among certain language users; at least, it cannot be excluded at the start.

Some philosophers talk of "the" concept of knowledge, but we should be open, at least in principle, to variability in specific concepts of knowledge employed by different people. The latter idea of specific concepts of knowledge seems to presume a univocal core in the various specific concepts, as they are all concepts of *knowledge*. Some philosophers will contend, however, that common *language*—for example, the linguistic term "knowledge"—is the only real core. We cannot settle this matter here, but it is noteworthy that variation in concepts used by some people in their descriptive and explanatory tasks does not entail variance in concepts *understood* by those people. You can understand a certain specific concept of knowledge, such as the one offered by a philosophy or psychology textbook, without employing it in your own descriptive and explanatory tasks. More generally, you can understand an author's definitions but refrain from adopting them in your own thinking and explaining. The important point, however, is that some people may use divergent specific concepts of knowledge, and we should be attentive to the possibility of such conceptual variation. As a result, a theory of knowledge may have to explain a variety of specific concepts of knowledge as well as a common general concept of knowledge underlying the various specific concepts. The subject matter of epistemology, in other words, may be conceptually diverse, at least at the level of specific concepts of knowledge.

What, then, is a theory of knowledge a theory *of*? That is, what kind of "thing" is knowledge, the subject matter of epistemology? Is it: (a) a natural kind (that is, a kind of thing in the world exemplifying stable properties susceptible to explanation and induction);

(b) a social construct; (c) an individual construct; or (d) something else? These questions are themselves matters of significant debate in the field of epistemology and hence resist easy answers. In addition, by what strategy, or method, are we to answer such questions? Can we answer such questions without relying on a theory of knowledge? If not, we may need to rely on a theory of knowledge, regardless of our preferred views on what exactly knowledge is. If knowledge is a natural kind, then epistemology will have a subject matter as objective as the subject matter of, say, biology or cognitive psychology. In that case, there will be a *correct* way, as opposed to an incorrect way, to explain what knowledge is, owing to the actual characteristics of knowledge.

We have just mentioned the epistemologist's aim to "explain what knowledge is." What exactly is this aim? Philosophers do not share a uniform answer. Since the time of Plato's *Meno* and *Theaetetus*, many epistemologists, in pursuit of explaining knowledge, have tried to formulate the essential components of human knowledge. In formulating these components, one will offer what contemporary philosophers call an "analysis" of (the concept of) knowledge. As suggested in Chapter 1, an influential traditional view, suggested by Plato (see *Meno* 97e–98a) and Kant among others, is that human propositional knowledge (that something is the case) has three individually necessary and jointly sufficient components: justification, truth, and belief. This view implies that human propositional knowledge is, by nature, justified true belief.

Epistemologists, as noted in Chapter 1, call the foregoing tripartite account the "traditional analysis" of knowledge. The justification condition requires that anyone who knows that P (where "P" stands for any proposition you like) have adequate justification, warrant, or evidential support for P. The truth condition requires that any known proposition be true rather than false, factual rather than erroneous. The belief condition requires that anyone who knows that P believe that P, having a psychological attitude of some confidence that P. The exact characterization of each of these proposed necessary conditions for knowledge is a matter of sustained dispute among epistemologists. We shall return to these conditions, and the issue of their sufficiency for knowledge, in Chapters 3 to 5.

EPISTEMOLOGY, NATURALISM, AND PRAGMATISM

Should any of us humans take the considerable time and trouble to formulate a philosophical explanation of human knowledge? If so, why? In the absence of decisive or widely accepted answers in epistemology, we might propose simply changing the subject. Perhaps philosophical explanations of knowledge are replaceable by the sciences or otherwise dispensable. Many people now seem inclined to think so, if only because philosophical disagreements about knowledge seem perennial, persistent without end.

Traditional epistemology of the sort found in Plato, Aristotle, Descartes, Locke (1632–1704), Kant, and Russell (1872–1970), among others, recommends a philosophical study of the nature, sources, and limits of knowledge. Two of its common background assumptions are that knowledge is roughly justified true belief and that epistemological assessment does not require (although it may include) distinctly scientific standards of evaluation. Some contemporary philosophers, including W. V. Quine and Richard Rorty, reject traditional epistemology.

Quine's rejection of traditional epistemology stems from his *replacement scientism*, the view that the sciences have a monopoly on legitimate theoretical explanation. Quine (1969) proposes that we should treat epistemology as a chapter of empirical psychology, that empirical psychology should exhaust the theoretical concerns of epistemologists. Call this bold proposal *replacement naturalism*. It implies that traditional epistemology is dispensable, being replaceable by empirical psychology. We may be tempted initially to say "Good riddance!" to traditional epistemology in light of its turbulent history of recurrent disagreements, but let's stave off that temptation for now.

Another prominent rejection of traditional epistemology stems from what we may call *replacement pragmatism*: the twofold view

that (a) the vocabulary, problems, and goals of traditional epistemology are unprofitable (not "useful") and thus in need of
replacement by pragmatist successors, and (b) the main task of
epistemology is to study the comparative advantages and disad-
vantages of the differing vocabularies from different cultures.
(For support of this position, see Rorty 1982.) Replacement pragmatism affirms the pointlessness and hence dispensability of
philosophical concerns about how the world really is (and about
objective truth), and recommends the central philosophical
importance of what is profitable, advantageous, or useful. Since
useful beliefs can be false — there were, after all, accurate calen-
dars based on a false astronomy before Copernicus — and
thereby fail to represent how the world really is, a desire for useful beliefs is not automatically a desire for beliefs representing
how the world really is. An obviously false belief can be useful to
a person with certain purposes. People often lie to others with
effective results.

Replacement pragmatism implies that a proposition is acceptable to us if and only if it is *useful* to us, that is, it is useful to us to
accept the proposition. (We may, if only for the sake of argument,
permit pragmatists to define "useful" however they find useful.)
If, however, usefulness determines acceptability in the manner
implied, a proposition will be acceptable to us if and only if it is
true (and thus *factually the case*) that the proposition is useful to
us. The pragmatist appeal to usefulness, therefore, entails something about matters of fact, or actual truth, regarding usefulness.
This is a *factuality requirement* on pragmatism. It manifests that
pragmatism does not — and evidently cannot — avoid considerations about the real, or factual, nature of things, about how things
really are.

Given the factuality requirement on pragmatism, we can easily
raise traditional epistemological questions about what is in fact
"useful." We can ask, for example, whether it is *true* that a particular proposition is useful to us, and whether we have adequate *evidence* that the proposition is useful. In addition, we can ask whether
we *know* that the proposition is useful, and even whether we are *certain* — say, in virtue of lacking any possible basis for doubt — that

the proposition is useful. Naturally, we must use intelligible epistemological notions in such questions, but this is no insurmountable obstacle, even by typical pragmatist standards. Hence, traditional epistemology, including its distinctive questions, can flourish even in an environment sustaining pragmatism. Traditional epistemology attracts no fatal challenge from pragmatism.

Replacement pragmatism itself faces a serious problem. Is it supposed to offer a *true* claim about acceptability? Does it aim to characterize the *real nature* of acceptability, how acceptability *really* is? If it does, it offers a characterization illicit by its own standard. It then runs afoul of its own assumption that we should eliminate from philosophy concerns about how things really are. As a result, replacement pragmatism faces a troublesome kind of self-defeat: It does what it says *should not* be done. In keeping with the previous remarks, we can also raise traditional epistemological questions about replacement pragmatism itself. For example, does replacement pragmatism actually make a *true* claim about acceptability? In addition, is its claim about acceptability knowable or even justifiable? Traditional epistemology can proceed smoothly on the basis of such questions.

If replacement pragmatism does not offer, or even aim to offer, a characterization of the real nature of acceptability, then why should we bother with it at all if we aim to characterize acceptability regarding propositions? Given the latter aim, we should not bother with it, for it is then irrelevant, *useless* to our purpose at hand. Considerations of usefulness, ever significant to pragmatism, can thus count against replacement pragmatism itself. A dilemma, then, confronts replacement pragmatism: Either replacement pragmatism is self-defeating or it is irrelevant to the typical epistemologist seeking an account of acceptability. This dilemma resists easy answers and indicates that replacement pragmatism fails to challenge traditional epistemology. Many epistemologists will not find a self-defeating theory "useful," given their explanatory aims. Accordingly, self-defeat will be troublesome for them, given the very standards of replacement pragmatism. It seems, then, that traditional epistemology can proceed with its central task of explaining human knowledge.

Replacement naturalism raises a problem similar to that facing replacement pragmatism. Such naturalism aims not for a mere description of our ordinary epistemological concepts, but rather for a kind of "explication" that, in the words of Rudolf Carnap, "consists in transforming a given more or less inexact concept into an exact one or, rather, in *replacing* the first by the second" (1950, p. 3; italics added). Aiming for such explication, replacement naturalists introduce conceptual *substitutes* for various ordinary epistemological and psychological concepts. Quine (1969) proposes, for instance, that we *replace* our ordinary notion of justification with a behaviorist notion concerning the relation between sensation and theory. He proposes, more generally, that replacement naturalists should regard the theory of knowledge as a branch of empirical psychology, while claiming that empirical psychology exhausts (and thus can replace) epistemology.

A natural objection is that replacement naturalism regarding epistemology is not itself a thesis of the sciences, including empirical psychology. Given this objection, replacement naturalism regarding epistemology evidently departs from Quine's own commitment to replacement scientism. Replacement scientism denies that there is any cognitively legitimate philosophy prior to, or independent of, the sciences (that is, any so-called "first philosophy"), thus implying that theorists should not make philosophical claims exceeding the sciences (see Quine 1954, p. 222; 1981, p. 21, for an identification of the domains of the scientific and the cognitive).

Quine's own replacement naturalism regarding epistemology — typically called his "naturalized epistemology"— seems to be an instance of philosophy prior to the sciences. Given this objection, Quine must show that his naturalized epistemology is an hypothesis of the sciences. Replacement naturalists may have difficulty discharging this burden, because the sciences seem not to be in the business of making sweeping claims about the status of epistemology (even if an individual scientist makes such claims on occasion). This may be an empirical truth about the sciences, but it is a warranted truth nonetheless, and it characterizes the sciences generally. Evidently, then, replacement naturalism regarding epistemology, as combined with replacement scientism, is self-defeating. A naturalist, of whatever stripe, should care to avoid self-defeat inasmuch as the sciences do and inasmuch as theoretical conflict is disadvantageous to unified explanation.

One might try to rescue replacement naturalism by proposing a notion of *science* broader than that underwritten by the sciences as standardly characterized. Such a proposal would perhaps relax the implied requirement that replacement naturalism be an hypothesis of the sciences. This, however, would place replacement naturalists on the horns of a troublesome dilemma: Either there will be *a priori* constraints on what counts as a science (because actual usage of "science" would not determine the broader notion), or the broader notion of science will be implausibly vague and unregulated in its employment. At a minimum, we need an account, in the absence of any standard independent of the sciences, of how we are to discern which of the various so-called sciences are regulative for purposes of theory formation in epistemology. Astrology, for example, will be out, and astronomy in. Such an account may very well take us beyond the sciences themselves, as it will be an account *of* the sciences, in particular, of their function in regulating epistemology.

To serve the purposes of replacement naturalism, any proposed new notion of science must exclude traditional epistemology, while including epistemological naturalism, in a way that is not *ad hoc*. Such a strategy for escaping self-defeat demands, in any case, a hitherto unexplicated notion of science, and this is no small order. Replacement naturalists have not defended any such strategy; nor have they otherwise resolved the aforementioned problem of self-defeat. That problem concerns only replacement naturalism, and not more moderate versions of epistemological naturalism in circulation. (See Goldman 1992 on some moderate versions of epistemological naturalism.)

Chapter 8 will return to the topic of replacement naturalism and introduce an alternative to it. In particular, it will propose that epistemology could have developed even if the empirical sciences, such as modern physics, chemistry, and biology, had not emerged. The reason for this, we shall see, is that the role of explanation in epistemology is intellectually general, and not dependent on features specific to the sciences. Various moderate versions of naturalism, in keeping with the sciences, likewise assign a special intellectual role to explanation, but they do not call for the replacement of epistemology by empirical psychology (even if epistemology is improved by the inclusion of our best psychology). The center of the contemporary debate over naturalist and non-naturalist approaches to epistemology is the issue whether epistemology is empirical rather than *a priori*.

In proposing the elimination of traditional epistemological categories, replacement naturalists typically appeal to the success of science in predicting and explaining significant aspects of the world. They assume that we, as explainers, should not adhere to the coarse and folksy conceptual scheme of belief, justification, and knowledge given that we can explain all that needs explaining by appeal to the sleek and technical categories of neuroscience and scientific psychology. Many philosophers have challenged the latter assumption. We have suggested that replacement naturalism is self-defeating, because it is itself an instance of philosophy prior to the sciences. More generally, debates about naturalism typically involve questions about "reductionism." Many reductive naturalists hold that the only real things in the world are the lower-level constituents (for example, electrons and protons) of higher-level phenomena (for example, individual humans and social groups). On their view, such terms as "belief" and "justification" involve just common-sense, practical ways of relating to a reality better characterized by the physical sciences. Many philosophers have argued, however, that most of science is profoundly antireductionist, both in practice and in principle. In keeping with this view, and with our argument concerning self-defeat, we see no plausible way to infer the elimination of epistemology merely from the success of the sciences.

Philip Kitcher (1992) has proposed the following core understanding of nonreplacement naturalistic epistemology:

1. The central problem of epistemology is to understand the epistemic quality of human cognitive performance, and to

specify strategies through whose use human beings can improve their cognitive states.

2. The epistemic status of a state is dependent on the processes that generate and sustain it.

3. The central epistemological project is to be carried out by describing processes that are reliable, in the sense that they would have a high frequency of generating epistemically virtuous states in human beings in our world.

4. Virtually nothing is knowable a priori, and, in particular, no epistemological principle is knowable a priori. (Pp. 74–76)

This book cannot make a final determination of the success of naturalistic epistemology as just characterized. The benefits and liabilities of naturalistic epistemology must be assessed in the light of technical meta-epistemological considerations that go beyond the scope of this book. Still, some general observations are appropriate.

Our adopting a naturalistic epistemology would affect the way we assess theories of knowledge and justification. For example, given a naturalistic epistemology implying that the causal basis of a belief is central to its justification, the assessment of justification will investigate complex *a posteriori* relations, ideally with the aid of our best empirical psychology. Some naturalists suggest that traditional nonnaturalist theories of knowledge are now in a position with respect to knowledge-relevant areas of psychology analogous to the meager position nineteenth-century metaphysics had with respect to matters concerning the chemical basis of life. Moderate naturalism, we have suggested, does not recommend the replacement of epistemology by physics, biology, or even psychology; that is, it does not entail replacement naturalism. Moderate naturalism preserves the traditional epistemological aim of formulating the most plausible explanation of human knowledge, both its structure and its sources. The relevant standards of explanation may include explanatory standards of intellectual inquiry in general, beyond strictly scientific criteria (for example, such standards as logical consistency, compatibility with total evidence, unification of different subject matters, and compatibility with our best sciences). Chapters 3, 6, and 7 will return to some psychological considerations pertinent to moderate naturalism in epistemology.

VALUE IN EPISTEMOLOGY

As traditionally practiced, epistemology seems inherently evaluative and hence normative, rather than just descriptive. It offers standards that evaluate some instances of belief as cases of genuine knowledge while excluding others from the category of genuine knowledge. Some recent debates about the meaning of "justification" revolve around the question whether, and if so how, the concept of epistemic (knowledge-relevant) justification is normative.

Since the 1950s Roderick Chisholm has defended the following "deontological" (that is, obligation-oriented) evaluative notion of justification: The claim that a proposition, *P*, is epistemically justified for you *means* that it is false that you ought to refrain from accepting *P*. In other words, to say that *P* is epistemically justified is to say that accepting *P* is *epistemically permissible*—at least in the sense that accepting *P* is consistent with a certain set of epistemic rules, or requirements. Typically such rules specify how one *ought* to acquire (informative) true belief and to avoid false belief. We might think of them as analogous to the rules of ethics concerning proper and improper action (see Chisholm 1989, pp. 59–60).

The deontological construal of justification enjoys some popularity in contemporary epistemology, and fits nicely with what philosophers call "the ethics of belief." It entails that a central part of epistemology concerns what kinds of beliefs are permissible and obligatory for humans in certain circumstances. The deontological approach offers an analogue in epistemology to our concern with permissible and obligatory actions in the familiar ethics of conduct. It does not, however, require that beliefs be under our *direct* control in the way many actions are. It requires only that belief formation be, in some way, indirectly controllable by us, perhaps in the way that many habits are under our indirect control.

We must be careful in formulating a deontological notion of justification. Suppose that you are raised in an isolated culture where all your available reliable sources report that dancing in a certain way causes rain to fall. Being in an isolated culture, you have no access to meteorological theory that challenges your sources' reports that dancing causes rain. Some people are inclined to grant that it would be epistemically permissible for you, in that situation, to believe that dancing in a certain way causes rain. Others will object that, in the absence of substantial evidence that dancing causes rain, you would not be epistemically justified in believing that dancing causes rain. It seems that a deontological approach to justification must be careful not to divorce epistemic justification from supporting evidence. Accordingly, such an approach must not confuse epistemically justified belief with *excusable* belief. A belief might be excusable even if it lacks supporting evidence. The kind of justification suitable to knowledge depends on adequate support from available evidence, and an excusable belief, within a certain context, may lack adequate support from available evidence. Excusable belief, we might say, is easier to come by than epistemically justified belief, even if it is difficult to specify exactly when support is "adequate." Contemporary epistemologists, as Chapter 5 will illustrate, dispute the exact conditions for adequate epistemic support.

A normative construal of justification need not be deontological, as it need not use a notion of obligation or permission in characterizing justification. William Alston (1985), for instance, has introduced a nondeontological normative concept of justification that relies mainly on the notion of what is *epistemically good* from the viewpoint of maximizing true belief and minimizing false belief. Such goodness need not be a matter of obligation (or, duty) or permissibility; it may be an evaluative matter independent of obligation and permissibility. Consider, for example, our claim that a certain athlete (say, Michael Jordan) is in "good" shape. Such a claim need not involve a statement about obligation or permissibility; it can be evaluative without being deontological.

Alston links epistemic goodness to a belief's being based on adequate grounds in the absence of overriding reasons to the contrary. A simple example is the case of your current belief that there are words on the page before you. Your belief is based on your current perceptual experience, and you have (we presume) no convincing challenges to this belief. The key notion of *adequate* grounds guarantees that the resulting epistemology will be evaluative and hence normative, even if not deontological. Epistemology may not be simply "ethics for the mind," but it does, in any case, standardly rely on evaluative notions exceeding mere description.

Let's grant that epistemology, as standardly practiced, is inherently evaluative and not merely descriptive. Two questions arise. First, do most of us really care about the kind of evaluative project called "epistemology"? Second, *should* we care, especially given all the other formidable demands on our time? It seems that many of us do care, inasmuch as we care about understanding the difference between genuine knowledge and merely apparent knowledge. We care about understanding the latter difference, because we care to grasp the distinction between recognizing effective means to our goals (whatever our goals are) and failing to recognize effective means to our goals.

Because failing to recognize means to our goals typically results in frustration of our goals, we ordinarily care to recognize effective means to our goals. In caring to recognize effective means to our goals, most of us likewise care to grasp the underlying distinction between genuinely recognizing effective means to our goals and merely *seeming* to recognize such means to our goals. We would not be satisfied, for example, with recognizing only means that merely *seem* to earn a college degree for us; we care about the real thing. To this extent, at least, most of us are inclined to care about the evaluative project called "epistemology."

Whether we "should" care about epistemology perhaps depends on our goals in life. Even so, as long as we have some goal in life (if only the higher-order goal not to have any first-order goals), epistemology will have value for us. We just noted that in caring to recognize effective means to our goals, most of us care to grasp the distinction between genuinely recognizing effective means to our goals and merely seeming to recognize such means to our goals. As a result, we should care about epistemology, at least insofar as epistemology sheds light on the relevant distinction between genuine knowledge (or, recognition) and merely apparent knowledge. We thus may conclude that epistemology is valuable at least for anyone who cares to recognize effective means to goals — even if epistemology does not supply a recipe for achieving all our particular goals. Because this may very well include all normal noninfant people, the value of epistemology is wide-ranging indeed. Very few, if any, other disciplines enjoy such breadth of demonstrable value.

Clearly, the value of epistemology transcends ordinary disciplinary lines. In any discipline in which knowledge is valuable, epistemology will contribute by way of elucidating the conditions, sources, and limits for genuine knowledge. Beyond philosophy proper (if one can ever get beyond philosophy), such disciplines as physics, chemistry, biology, anthropology, psychology, sociology, and theology will benefit from epistemology, at least insofar as they value genuine knowledge of some species or other. Epistemology is not the final arbiter of specific disputes in those disciplines. For example, traditional epistemologists are not the appropriate judges of specific theoretical disputes about the techniques used in the Human Genome Project. Still, epistemology can make a significant contribution by way of clarifying relevant notions of knowledge and justification and the corresponding principles that can be used to identify genuine knowledge and justification. Epistemology, then, is by no means just for philosophers. It's a vital discipline for anyone pursuing cognitive projects — or any projects, for that matter.

We have seen that a theory of knowledge raises a number of difficult questions about the nature of its own subject matter. Answers to these questions will vary among theories of knowledge, but it does not follow that every answer is as defensible as any other. Divergent answers in epistemology can include untenable and even false members. We should resist, then, the view that epistemological disagreement entails an "anything goes" attitude toward knowledge or theories thereof. It is noteworthy, in any case, that proponents of an "anything goes" attitude rarely take such an attitude toward their "anything goes" attitude itself. Chapter 4 will return to the topic of relativism about truth.

In sum, then, we have identified some important debates about the nature of the concept of knowledge, and we have argued that epistemology is indeed indispensable. Traditional epistemology, we have suggested, is not replaceable by either the sciences (contrary to replacement naturalism) or the study of what is useful to us (contrary to replacement pragmatism). We have also demonstrated the value of epistemology for any person with any definite goals. Epistemology is an evaluative discipline of central importance to any human with goals. We turn now to the belief component of knowledge.

3

Belief

Beliefs fill our minds, for better or worse. Beyond ordinary perceptual beliefs, we have scientific, moral, political, and theological beliefs. If the traditional analysis of knowledge is correct, then
belief is a necessary condition for knowledge. Described thus,
belief may appear to be a simple logical feature of knowledge,
and this may explain why many traditional epistemologists have
not explored belief as a complex psychological state. Instead,
they have treated belief as a monolithic state that can take a mul-
titude of propositions as objects. Given the traditional analysis, if
you don't understand to some extent what belief is, you likewise
don't understand what knowledge is. So, belief merits careful
attention from a theory of knowledge.

This chapter will examine several features of belief that are
central to its epistemic roles. It will emerge that the premium
placed on a philosophically general analysis of knowledge has
produced a rarified and abstract account of belief (along with justification), and in so doing has failed to capture not only epistemologically important differences between various cognitive

states but also similarly important relations between epistemology and psychology.

BELIEF AND REPRESENTATIONAL STATES

A belief, at least as we ordinarily use the term, is *about* some state of affairs. In virtue of this property of "aboutness," a state is *intentional* or, more generically, has *meaning*. In the same way that the meaning of a sentence is supplied by the proposition it expresses, the meaning of a mental state such as a belief is provided by the state of affairs, or the proposition, that would have to be the case for the belief to be true. Given this intentional feature, beliefs are *representational*, functioning as maps by which we portray and navigate the world (see Armstrong 1973, chap. 1).

One prominent view in the philosophy of mind has clear epistemological import. According to this view, each of the "propositional attitudes," as philosophers call such psychological states as belief, desire, hope, and fear, is fully specified by two features: psychological relation and propositional content. Consider a mental state regarding, for example, the superior status of mastiffs as pets. Such a state would be an attitude of belief in virtue of the *nature* of the psychological relation you bear to the proposition that mastiffs are superior pets. You can, of course, have different attitudes toward the same proposition. You can believe, desire, hope, or fear that mastiffs are superior pets. The differences between such propositional attitudes are reflected in the ways you think about and act toward mastiffs. If you merely *desired* (rather than believed) that mastiffs were superior pets, you would not necessarily try to convince others of this, or want to buy a mastiff (all other things being equal).

In addition, any psychological relation (belief, desire, fear, etc.) can have various propositions as objects. You can have the belief that mastiffs are superior pets, that the racehorse Ernie R. is a mudder, that Hieronymus Bosch's painting *Garden of Earthly Delights* is profoundly apocalyptic rather than pagan, or that Bosch makes high-performance spark plugs. It is not the propositional attitude that would make such mental states different; it is rather the relevant propositional *content*, the propositions to which the (in this case, belief) attitude is related.

In traditional epistemology, philosophers have sometimes taken belief to be an all-or-nothing matter: Either you believe that *P* or you don't. This seems at best an idealization, an oversimplification that contributes to ease of analysis. Looking at actual cases of epistemic commitment, we find that they vary in both *degree* and *relation*. Variation in degree, by itself, poses no problem for the supposition that the notion of belief is clear. We can have varying degrees of confidence; in particular, we can be more or less confident about the truth of some proposition. Your not being confident in your *belief* that mastiffs are prone to tumors does not entail that there is some other psychological relation you bear to that proposition, for example, the *fear* that mastiffs are prone to tumors, or the *hope* that they are not. Your confidence does bear, however, on the likelihood you (would) assign to a proposition believed.

Much of contemporary epistemology emerged during the 1960s and 1970s, a period that produced voluminous and subtle analyses of justification and knowledge. Although much effort focused on intricate counterexamples to analyses of the justification condition, far less effort concerned the notion of belief. Much of the seminal literature treated belief as a fairly undifferentiated notion, and included only those distinctions of belief status that could be appreciated from casual philosophical inspection. So, while there can be as many particular beliefs as there are *possible objects* of belief, the sense in which one might believe any of these propositional objects did not vary significantly among epistemological analyses.

Recently, philosophers and psychologists have studied belief in its various cognitive roles: in attitude formation, induction, contribution to bias, and a host of other psychological processes. The virtual consensus now is that beliefs are information-bearing states of a special sort. The kind of information beliefs bear depends, at least in part, on the way they represent the world. If a belief represents the world inaccurately — if it misrepresents the world — the belief is false. If, in contrast, a belief represents the world aright, it is true, or factual. As just suggested, not all mental states are beliefs. We have desires, hopes, fears, and other propositional states as well. All such states are representational in that they supply a kind of map, or scenario, of some part of the world. For example, to fear that there is a snake in the grass is to fear that the world is a certain way — that it is such that there is a snake in the grass. Representation is an indispensable ingredient of our mental lives.

Some mental states are not representational, and so may have a different epistemological role from beliefs. Consider, for example, so-called nonpropositional qualitative states, such as the auditory experiences we have when listening to a piano recital or the color sensations we experience while pressing the heels of our hands into our closed eyes. The latter states are not necessarily *about* anything. The neural processes that underlie or realize these qualitative states may be causally connected to the world. Even so, it seems doubtful that this would make the experiential content of the aforementioned color sensations, for instance, representational in the way that belief is.

Our nonpropositional qualitative experiences might seem different from typical beliefs in that such experiences are, in the language of some philosophers, incorrigible: Evidently, we cannot be mistaken about their contents. This incorrigibility thesis holds, however, only in the sense that no judgment whatever is involved as an object of such experiences. You have a sensation of loud noise when you pound on the piano keys. You could be right or wrong about the judgment *that* the noise is loud, but the sensation itself cannot be mistaken (or accurate) because it is not a judgment.

Beliefs are inherently propositional, requiring some propositional object or other. Beliefs are not, however, psychological actions or occurrent episodes; they are representational psychological *states* that may or may not be manifested in overt behavior. You can believe that 2 + 2 = 4, for instance, while *doing* nothing at all, or at least while being sound asleep with no thought of arithmetic. Beliefs seem akin to some habits we have, in that they involve *tendencies* to behave in certain ways under certain circumstances. In the case of beliefs, the relevant tendency, being representational, seems to be a disposition to assent to certain propositional content under suitable circumstances. The assenting in question is itself episodic, being an action, but it need not be manifested in overt behavior. Because you can believe something now without assenting to it now (recall your being sound asleep while believing that $2 + 2 = 4$), belief is not identical with an action of assenting.

Although our ordinary use of "belief" is rather vague and thus leaves many cases of possible belief undecided, we should not let that trouble us now. We are interested in the cognitive role of belief, and it is no serious objection to the claim that belief has an important cognitive function that our notion of belief sometimes leaves it unclear whether a person believes a particular proposition. Some philosophers have argued that this sort of vagueness is incompatible with a scientifically acceptable state. Their argument gets its force from the apparently holistic character of belief ascriptions.

In an influential example, Stephen Stich (1983, pp. 54–56) asks us to consider Mrs. T, who at one time believed that McKinley was assassinated, but has since suffered progressive memory loss. She is not sure what the term "assassination" means, and remembers the name "McKinley," but does not recall a President by that name. Does she really believe that McKinley was assassinated? Perhaps not. By imagining a slightly better memory and a more secure grasp of relevant concepts, however, we can see how beliefs may be graded. Clearly, and fortunately, people can have unclarity of belief without being pathological. A child, for example, can believe that her father's brother is her uncle, even if she doesn't fully grasp all the relevant kinship notions. We would have very few beliefs indeed if belief required full comprehension of all constituent notions.

BELIEF AND BELIEF ASCRIPTION

We should distinguish between belief and its attribution, that is, between belief and belief ascription. Attribution of belief is a pragmatic procedure in that it is something we do with language, particularly the language of belief. Some lenient purposes for which we attribute the belief that *P* to a person do not require that the person possess all the concepts central to the belief that *P*. For example, you might ascribe to a baby the belief that the nearby radiator is hot, even though you would grant that the baby lacks any concept of radiator. We thus should not conclude simply from a useful tendency to attribute beliefs *as if* they were held by certain people that they are actually held by those people. Usefulness of belief ascription is not automatically evidence of genuine belief. Belief is one thing; useful belief ascription, another. Similarly, we should not conclude from a useful tendency to ascribe beliefs *as if they were true* that the beliefs ascribed are themselves actually held or even *actually true*. Our ascribing beliefs seemingly true by our lights does not guarantee that the beliefs thereby ascribed are actually held by others or are actually true. Needless to say, the world does not always comply with beliefs that seem true.

As a policy of belief ascription, the Principle of Charity states that we must ascribe to our interlocutors beliefs that are mostly true. The Principle is epistemologically important because some philosophers have used it to argue against skepticism. In particular, Donald Davidson has argued that skepticism must be false because the Principle of Charity is true. Regardless of whether we use the Principle in ordinary interpretive practice, including when we interpret people from very different cultures, the Principle abets a philosophical misunderstanding we need to identify.

The attribution of beliefs and preferences to others, including others from a radically different culture, challenges us to translate the utterances of others into language we can understand. In this connection, the Principle of Charity offers a ready method of rationalizing explanation. Historians and clinical psychologists face the same interpretive problem as anthropologists — to describe and render intelligible the behavior of other, sometimes radically different, agents. Philosophers sympathetic with the Principle argue that the pressures of understanding favor a method of interpretation that "puts the interpreter in general agreement with the speaker" (Davidson 1980, p. 169).

Charitable interpretation is not a *choice* we make, according to Davidson. Rather, Davidson proposes, "charity is forced upon us; whether we like it or not, if we want to understand others, we must count them right in most matters" (1980, p. 197). Under the strain of disagreement, however, the interpreter trumps the speaker. Whoever is doing the interpreting, according to Davidson, gets to say who is right. If we are the interpreters, of course, this eases the burden of charity for us. As long as we are earnest interpreters, given the Principle of Charity, our interpretive provincialism requires no apology. Even an omniscient interpreter, according to Davidson, "attributes beliefs to others, and interprets their speech on the basis of his own beliefs, just as the rest of us do" (1980, p. 201).

The Principle of Charity is by no means a piece of received philosophical wisdom. Many philosophers reject it, claiming that sensitive interpretation at times requires that we find others mistaken in most matters, and that there is no special number of false beliefs that precludes our interpreting the behavior of others intelligibly. The task of interpreting behavior is explanatory, and if the best explanation of another's behavior requires the attribution of mostly false beliefs, then so be it. At least, we cannot preclude this option *a priori*. In any case, the Principle of Charity does little, by itself, to undermine the threat of skepticism, because it could be true that we must ascribe beliefs *as though* the person's beliefs are mostly true, even if the beliefs in question are not actually mostly true. It seems doubtful, then, that the Principle of Charity illuminates either the nature of belief or the problem of skepticism.

ARE BELIEFS TRANSPARENT?

Epistemology concerns not just our knowledge of others, but also our knowledge of ourselves, and thereby involves the character of self-knowledge. Many philosophers have commented on the difficulty of knowing the contents of one's own thoughts, and some, such as Kant, have even argued that we come to know the contents of our own minds in the same way we come to know any other empirical fact. As a result, we can be mistaken in our beliefs about what motivated us in a particular case. In short, then, when self-ascribed beliefs constitute knowledge, it is because they are (approximately) true and justified. Here, too, truth and justification matter to knowledge.

Some philosophers have proposed that our mental states are immediately introspectible — a view sometimes called *the transparency thesis.* According to this view, we can know what we believe simply by looking inward, as it were, by immediately observing the contents of our minds. According to Descartes ([1640]): "Nothing can be in me, that is to say, in my mind, of which I am not aware." (Some commentators on Descartes hold that he restricted his transparency thesis to *occurrent* mental states, but we shall not digress to the vicissitudes of Descartes exegesis; our focus is on positions, not figures.) In addition, George Berkeley thought that a demonstration that a mental state was not present emerged from the fact that the thinker was not aware of it: "Every one is himself the best judge of what he perceives, and what not. In vain shall all the mathematicians in the world tell me that I perceive certain *lines* and *angles* which introduce into my mind the various *ideas* of *distance*, so long as I myself am conscious of no such thing" ([1709], para. 12).

Several considerations tell against any strong version of the transparency thesis. First, sometimes the best explanation of our behavior requires the attribution of an attitude to us that is not immediately introspectible by us. The view that we can have mental states not immediately introspectible by us demands no indulgence of psychoanalysis and no assumption that a third party is better positioned to know our mental states than we are. Rather, the view asserts that some intentional states needed to explain important psychological behavior are not immediately accessible to the subject of those states. Second, some intentional states important in psychological processing cannot be accessed at will, and we are not aware of them as they are operative. These states are sometimes called *subdoxastic,* and we shall return to them soon. Third, if beliefs are dispositional states rather than actions, then it should be no real surprise that we can have beliefs not immediately introspectible by us. After all, a dispositional state, like a habit, can exist while being unmanifested.

Let's reflect on the first consideration against the extreme transparency thesis. According to a prominent psychological tradition, we can have unconscious mental states. Freud famously thought, and many theorists before him held, that much of our behavior could be adequately explained only via appeal to unconscious desires and beliefs. You may not consciously contrive to delay your appointments with a colleague you find unpleasant, but you nonetheless keep showing up late. If such tardiness is uncharacteristic of you, then an unconscious desire to avoid the colleague may be part of the best explanation of your behaving as you do. Such an explanation would imply no specific psychoanalytic theory. So, we can accept the claim that we have unconscious mental states while rejecting nearly everything Freud, Adler, or Jung said about them. In any case, the important point is that we lack reason to think that all of our unconscious mental states are immediately introspectible by us.

As for the second consideration against transparency, consider psychological states that are *subdoxastic*. Such states reflect cognitive convictions of a special sort. Stich (1978) has argued that the distinction between ordinary psychological states and those "subpersonal" or "subdoxastic" states successfully studied in cognitive psychology is marked by two characteristics. Subdoxastic states, represented, for example, in E. H. Hess's (1975) pupillary diameter study, are distinguished from ordinary belief states by their *inferential isolation* and their *inaccessibility to consciousness*. In Hess's experiment, male subjects were presented with almost identical photos of a woman. One of the photos was retouched, however, making the woman's pupils slightly larger than in the other photo. Subjects regularly reported finding the woman in the retouched photo more attractive, even though they were not able to explain why or to identify the relevant difference between the two photos. Because there is undoubtedly some mechanism that processes information about pupillary diameter and responds to a difference in pupillary diameter (which is curiously inexpressible in the casually queried subject), we can see the rationale for claiming that some states underlying the production of a belief are inaccessible to consciousness.

Although subdoxastic states can serve as premises for inferences to beliefs, they are not (to use Stich's expression) "inferentially promiscuous" in the way ordinary beliefs are. Consciously accessible beliefs are potentially inferentially related to a vast range of other beliefs; that is, they can stand in inference relations to beliefs involving virtually any topic. By contrast, the inferential routes relating subdoxastic states to beliefs are specialized and limited. Only a narrow range of beliefs (say, visual beliefs of a certain kind), can be arrived at from a particular subdoxastic state. Stich's description of the processes operating on subdoxastic states as "specialized and limited" anticipates Jerry Fodor's influential description of psychological modules as "highly specialized computational mechanisms" (see Fodor 1983).

Evidently, then, explanations within specific areas of experimental psychology use a different notion of psychological state from that used in common sense, or "folk," explanations. It would be inaccurate to explain a subject's description of the woman in the retouched photo as "more attractive" in terms of his belief that women with larger pupils are more attractive. Once we give up the idea that the contents of our epistemic commitments must be immediately introspectible, or transparent, to us, we can acknowledge as psychologically important exactly those states that figure centrally in our best contemporary theories of perception and cognition.

BELIEF AND THEORETICAL IDEALS

Epistemological talk is, of course, full of idealization. We describe beliefs simply as justified or unjustified, even though justification doubtless comes in degrees. Another important idealization in contemporary epistemology is the unqualified reference to "true" belief. In fact, many beliefs counted as knowledge are not strictly true; they are only *approximately* true. We often make knowledge claims (sometimes only implicitly formulated as such) about our height or weight, for instance, and we seldom know those values *exactly.* (This holds even if we overlook typical rounding off in our favor.) Similarly, if all you want to do is fit your house with new storm windows, you don't have to measure the window opening to the micron, even if you could; rather, measurement to a quarter of an inch will do just fine, even for what will qualify as factual knowledge. It is, however a skeptic's routine ploy to parlay this inaccuracy into global epistemological pessimism.

For those who deem the skeptic to be insincere, inconsistent, or ill-informed (issues of sanity aside), there is a rationale for counting some claims of imperfect accuracy among legitimate cases of factual knowledge: Given the intellectual goals at hand, the claims are adequately justified; moreover, they are suitably, if imprecisely, true. Indeed, given the typical purposes of measurement, there are two reasons why it would be epistemologically irresponsible to claim that an *approximately* true assertion is not *really* true. First, like the prohibition on unnecessary significant figures in measurement generally, it is misleading to present estimation to the nearest micron as more accurate than estimation to the nearest inch if there is no difference in the reliability of those estimates given the imprecision of the instruments used or the permissiveness of the goals pursued. Second, accuracy is typically achieved at the expense of greater time, expense, and effort. It would be irresponsible to demand such accuracy if you get nothing at all for it.

The pragmatic, or context-sensitive, feature of knowledge manifests a lesson about the theory dependence of justification: Our theoretical purposes, or goals, determine what degree of support or reliability is required for a belief to be justified. (For some support for this lesson, see Helm 1994.) If we want simply to estimate the velocity of a molecule in an enclosed volume of gas, we need not worry that the container's proximity to the sun changes from season to season. Gravitational influences on the molecule, though real, are irrelevant to the theoretical purposes of measuring its velocity (given the pressure of the gas). In epistemology, as in physics, this similarity judgment is theory dependent. We rely on a theory when we judge that the position of the moon is irrelevant to the justification of my belief that there is a tree in front of me.

A prominent theme in this book concerns the philosophical influences on a chosen epistemological view. An eliminativist about our ordinary notion of belief, such as W. V. Quine (1954) or Paul Churchland (1989), will not have much patience for an epistemological view that centrally features our ordinary notion of belief. The same goes for the radical behaviorist psychologist.

The position of logical behaviorism, common in the 1950s and 1960s, has been roundly refuted since then. (This involves a striking development in the philosophy of mind that falls beyond the scope of this book; see Gardner 1987 for the details and Fodor 1981 for a survey of relevant positions). Logical behaviorism is pertinent here, however, for two reasons. First, it represents the way in which one's philosophical views in one area depend on one's philosophical views in another. Many philosophers have noted that logical behaviorists' demand that mental-state words (such as "belief" and "desire") be defined in terms of observable behavior is a vestige of a more broadly empiricist (that is, experience-based) account of definition and meaning. The moral: Expect logical behaviorists to have an empiricist account of justification and, in general, expect definite thematic connections among a philosopher's various views. In this respect, philosophy is irredeemably holistic.

The second reason for mentioning logical behaviorism concerns the general position we have suggested about the nature of belief. Throughout, we have relied on the idea that a belief is a mental representation. Commitment to an unobservable internal state such as a mental representation is, however, likely to leave logical behaviorists squeamish, and it may have the same effect on some other philosophers, including some eliminative materialists.

Eliminativists about intentional states need not deny that it is *useful* to ascribe intentional states. They rather deny that such attributions are *true*. It is difficult, however, to reconcile eliminativism about belief with the impressive results of perceptual, cognitive, and social psychology. As long as we are careful to distinguish genuine belief from the grounds for ascribing belief, we can offer a way of establishing that someone has a belief: If a person believes that P, then that person would assent to the proposition that P under suitable conditions (which include, for instance, absence of an intention to deceive regarding what is believed). Use of this criterion will be fallible, and it does not offer a full definition of the term "belief." Someone can always refuse to assent to a statement for any reason he or she finds sufficiently compelling. For example, a person can seek to deceive others about his or her actual beliefs. Even so, if a person believes that P, then that person would assent to the proposition that P under suitable conditions.

If belief incorporates the previous sort of tendency, or disposition, to assent to a proposition, we can naturally ask how many other beliefs we have in virtue of having a particular belief. If you believe the laws of mathematics, do you also believe all the logical consequences of those laws, that is, the consequences required by the laws of logic? We believe that 63 divided by 9 equals 7. We believe this in virtue of certain relations that we believe hold between division, multiplication, and the number system. Do we thereby also believe that $15,346 \times 241 = 3,698,386$? If yes, we believe statements we would not necessarily be inclined immediately to assent to. If no, we need an explanation of when we actually do believe the logical consequences of our beliefs.

Although our example is mathematical, the phenomenon of tacit, or implicit, belief is quite general. No psychoanalytic interpretation is required here. We can hold that some beliefs are beneath the threshold of conscious scrutiny, without thereby holding that these beliefs are forever repressed in the absence of a psychoanalyst's firm guidance. Rather, there are various reasons why beliefs may play a causal role in producing our behavior (or in interacting with other mental states such as fears and desires) even though we are not directly aware of their presence. Even so, the supposition that we believe all the deductive consequences of our beliefs has some counterintuitive implications. Some philosophers favoring this view simply bite the bullet and claim that we have an infinity of beliefs. Others seek a clear way to distinguish a mere disposition to believe that *P* from a genuine belief that *P*.

We need not settle the complicated issue of the exact defining conditions of belief. The plausibility of an answer to such a complex issue is seldom judged on the basis of any simple intuition. Rather, such plausibility is typically addressed by appeal to general theoretical views. For present purposes, the important point is twofold: Beliefs are dispositional and representational, and we appear to have cognitive states with representational contents not transparent to us, not immediately introspectible. One cause of this limit on introspection derives from the fact that we can process only a limited amount of information in a given period of time, while many events both from within and without compete for our attention. Were we to claim that only occurrent (or episodic) beliefs are genuine, we would be in the uncomfortable position of holding that many apparently important belief states in our cognitive lives are not genuine beliefs at all.

ELIMINATIVISM AND PREDICTION

We have touched on a position that takes various forms in recent philosophy: eliminativism about belief. Eliminativist philosophers hold that our beliefs are brain states and that we shall someday discover that there is nothing even like belief as we currently conceive it. Appeals to belief in psychological and epistemological discourse, eliminativist philosophers predict, will be eliminated in favor of appeals to neural states of theoretically important sorts. On this view, epistemology will be redefined as, or at least replaced by, a branch of neuroscience.

Two reasons recommend against endorsement of eliminativism in its current form. First, it is unclear what exactly is being predicted by eliminativism. That is, it is not clear what would be required for us to find that "there are no beliefs." In particular, eliminativist philosophers have not offered a very well-developed account of radical reduction — an account stating when one theory entirely displaces another, and when one theory actually ratifies the existence of another theory's objects. Second, the main prediction by eliminativism remains unconfirmed. Fascinating developments in cognitive neuroscience have in no way stunted or made dispensable advances in areas of psychology clearly relying on our ordinary notion of belief, areas such as cognitive and social psychology. (For some of these developments, see Goldman 1986, 1992.)

Like the question of whether eliminativism is true, the question of whether the ordinary, or folk, notion of belief has a secure place in a scientific psychology is an empirical one capable of support or disconfirmation on empirical grounds. Even so, some philosophers have tried to argue, without appeal to empirical evidence, that eliminativism is inconsistent and false. According to their argument, eliminativists commit "cognitive suicide" given that statements asserting *belief* in eliminativism are, by the very standards of eliminativism, self-defeating. Because there are no beliefs if eliminativism is true, eliminativists cannot consistently claim that they *believe* that eliminativism is true. By focusing on the logical structure of eliminativist claims, some philosophers thus criticize eliminativism independently of the empirical evidence that might confirm or disconfirm it.

Self-defeat arguments rely, for their cogency, on an accurate reconstruction of the position under attack, and when they lack such a reconstruction, the targeted position can evade trouble. In this case, eliminativists claim that eliminativism *predicts* that the truth of eliminativism will outstrip the ability of folk notions to express it. According to eliminativists, belief is not a theoretical kind of a mature scientific vocabulary. Even if we now lack an adequate successor to the vocabulary of belief, it does not follow that the vocabulary of belief accurately reflects our most trustworthy theoretical commitments. All that follows is that sometimes our only available vocabulary (in this case, the vocabulary of belief) is misleading. A new neuroscientific theory may someday supply a vocabulary expressing new cognitive notions and new neural notions that jointly replace the folk notion of belief. If such neuroscientific notions appear, according to eliminativists, we ought to decide whether eliminativism is warranted, and whether folk psychology is disconfirmed, on the enhanced empirical evidence.

Critics of eliminativism should acknowledge the predictive status of eliminativism, and assess the position accordingly. Two problems are outstanding. First, we lack adequate grounds now for reasonable confidence that the promissory notes of eliminativism will be satisfied by future science. Predictions of the future of science are dangerous business indeed, and we can now reasonably refrain from commitment to eliminativist predictions. Second, we can now reasonably regulate our cognitive theories by our *current* evidence, and our current evidence does not call for elimination of the notion of belief. Our evidence may, of course, change, but it would be rash indeed to formulate current theory on the basis of a sweeping prediction about how exactly it will change.

The earlier description of subdoxastic states made clear that scientific psychology plays an important role in an epistemological theory. Philosophers have been concerned to delineate general epistemological notions such as belief and justification, but psychologists have specified, at least to some extent, the actual mechanisms responsible for the formation and justification of beliefs. Chapters 8 and 9 will consider the epistemological role for philosophy once epistemological notions are influenced by systematic empirical inquiry.

Given our best empirical evidence, we should note that the capacity to believe is not restricted to humans. Any animal that can represent and misrepresent the world is a candidate believer. It is not, however, always an easy task to identify a candidate knower, no matter how blithely we use intentional vocabulary to describe animal behavior. Some bees do a "dance" to communicate to other bees the direction of a nectar source. To avoid attack, a hognose snake feigns death and, as part of the drama, is able to exude blood from a special gland. Many ground-nesting birds protect their young from prey by feigning injury, drawing the predator's attention away from the young in the nest. Do these animals have beliefs? Does the adult plover's broken-wing display arise from its *belief* that if the predator believes the plover is injured, then the predator will pursue the adult plover rather than the chicks?

Chapter 6 will introduce the idea that some knowledge is innate. To credit the plover with genuinely intelligent behavior, we need to know whether the plover simply executes this routine independently of genuine threat to its chick. In short, intelligent behavior is typically behaviorally *flexible*. If automated behavior is not epistemically interesting, then it would be important to determine whether the plover can't act otherwise, and whether the same behavior can be mechanically prompted in a wide range of conditions. The key to answering whether some nonhuman animals have beliefs seems to lie in the flexibility of the behavior. If the behavior is flexible, then perhaps the animal is able to *represent* different ways that the world could be. An empirical research program aims to determine what exactly the relevant flexibility consists in.

It is a separate question whether we may evaluate all animal beliefs in terms of justification. According to the traditional analysis of knowledge, whether animals can have propositional knowledge depends on whether their beliefs can be justified. Propositional knowledge, according to this analysis, requires justified true belief. The key assumption of this chapter is that propositional knowledge, as traditionally understood, requires the kind of representational state that we call "belief." Belief is, however, a psychologically complex phenomenon, and it is one task of cognitive psychology to characterize exactly how belief functions. In this respect, at least, epistemology benefits from the lessons of psychology.

In sum, then, we have seen that beliefs are inherently representational and that they should not be confused with mere ascriptions of beliefs. As dispositional states, our beliefs are not always immediately accessible to us, but this lack of transparency does not challenge the reality of beliefs. We have found no reason to favor eliminativism about beliefs; in fact, we have expressed doubts about the eliminativist prediction that our best science will dispense with talk of beliefs. Having sketched the nature of belief, we can turn to the next essential condition for knowledge: the truth condition.

4

Truth

The previous chapter examined the nature of belief because belief is a prerequisite for knowledge. To know that P (for any proposition, P), we must believe that P. The next essential condition for knowledge is truth. We know that P only if P is true. Some people object, after first hearing this restriction on knowledge. They think about people in the past who believed, for example, that the earth is stationary at the center of the universe. They realize that many of our ancestors had no indication that the earth is moving at a considerable velocity through space. These people think that because our ancestors had no sign of the earth's motion and were hence responsible and rational in their belief, we should honor and respect their rationality by giving their belief the honorific label "knowledge." They hold that, because our ancestors were rational, and because we would have believed the same thing had we been in their place, our ancestors should not be denied their claim to knowledge.

In keeping with a lesson of Chapter 1, the denial of our ancestors' claims to know that the earth is stationary is not a criticism of *them* or an indictment of their rationality. They might have attended to all the available evidence with due care and formed their beliefs in an epistemically responsible way. It simply turns out that they were wrong, and that is not very unusual for human believers. Their belief was justified on the basis of their best available evidence, we can acknowledge, even though it is a false belief. Chapter 5 will consider some accounts of how such beliefs could have been justified, but now we should note that a belief's being *false* does not entail that it is *unjustified*. Our ancestors had, and we presumably have, many justified false beliefs, and these fail to qualify as knowledge owing to their falsity.

This chapter addresses the question of what truth is. To many, this sounds like an unmanageably deep philosophical question, calling for ponderous but inconclusive reflection. Facing the weighty question, "What is truth?," many theorists feel overwhelmed, at a loss for any significant response. The Truth (with a big "T") deserves reverence and awe but not analysis, according to these theorists. For many others, in contrast, the question does not have such a profound air but appears as a more tangible, although still difficult, question. It is tied up closely with questions about how sentences or statements in a language can be true and questions about how propositional attitudes called beliefs can be true. Our question is akin to the general question of how language becomes meaningful in such a way that it can refer to things in the world, and to the question of how we can represent in our minds assertions about the world and hence the world itself. When asking about truth, we are specifically interested in finding what conditions a sentence, statement, belief, or proposition must satisfy to be true.

Like most contemporary epistemologists, we favor the second of the two aforementioned approaches to the question of truth. At the very least, the second approach is preferable because it gives us some idea of how to proceed toward a satisfactory answer to the question of what truth is. The first approach to the question of truth leaves us wondering how we should even get started in treating our question. We are thereby left gaping at an apparently unapproachable mystery. Philosophers, given their role as explainers, should remove such mystery whenever appropriate.

RELATIVISM

Chapter 1 dealt briefly with the topic of relativism about truth. It pointed out that relativism about truth, rather than supporting skepticism about knowledge, really makes knowledge fairly easily acquirable. The idea that truth is relative is, needless to say, popular in many circles. Some people are fond of saying, for example, that it was *true for* many societies of the past that the earth is stationary at the center of the universe. We have also mentioned the example of someone who claims that the proposition "God exists" is *true for* the believer but *not true for* the nonbeliever. What do such relativist claims really amount to? What is it for something to be *true for* a person, rather than simply *true*? Attention to these questions will shed light on relativism about truth.

The relativist's thesis might easily be confused with the claim that people can, in some sense, make their own truth. The latter claim is vague and ambiguous, but there is at least one interpretation that makes it an obviously correct claim. We all have the power, a limited power, to make some things true. For example, if the window is open and I am cold, I have the power to "create" the truth of the window's being closed; I get up and close the window. The sentence "The window is closed" was false, but I make it true by closing the window. (Many philosophers would add a word of caution here about how to handle changing truth values, but we need not worry about this now.) In some sense, then, we can "make our own truth" or "make our own reality," but this is just a flowery—and potentially misleading—way of saying that we have some power to influence our surroundings. This mundane point should not be confused with the more controversial claims of the relativist about truth. Some things, we must acknowledge, are not within our power.

The relativist's stronger claim would be, for example, that it could be true *for me* that the window is open while at the same time it is false *for you* that the window is open. Many people mistake this for the more modest claim that it can *appear to me* that the window is open while at the same time it *appears to you* that the window is closed. This more modest claim is hardly controversial, for it is quite clear that the same thing can appear in different ways to different people, depending, for example, on their differing perspectives, their differing powers of perception, and so forth. This more modest claim is *not* the relativist thesis.

A closely related point likewise fails to capture the relativist thesis. Philosophers widely agree that rational belief can be relative in the sense that one person in one situation can rationally believe what would be irrational for another person in a different situation to believe. One person can have evidence to support a belief while another person lacks evidence for that same belief. So, the first person could justifiably believe what the second person may not justifiably believe. The belief is *justified for person A* while it is *unjustified for person B*, but this is not the same as saying that a belief is *true for A* while being *false for B*.

The relativist about truth might be claiming that somehow the standards that one uses for *determining*, or *identifying*, what is true actually constitute what it is to *be* true. This involves an important distinction. On the one hand, we can discuss what it is to *be true*. That is, we can discuss what the defining conditions are under which a belief or statement is true. On the other hand, we can discuss what methods a person should employ for *discerning*, or *identifying*, what beliefs and statements are true. These are the methods, or rules, one would use for trying to find, or pick out, the beliefs and statements that satisfy the defining conditions for being true.

By way of analogy, consider the distinction we make between the defining conditions for *being* a dollar bill and the standards we use for *identifying* dollar bills. We identify dollar bills mainly on the basis of their appearance. We look for the picture of George Washington, the 1's, the label "Federal Reserve Note," the seal of the Treasury Department, and so on. For something to *be* a dollar bill, however, it needs more than just these superficial characteristics. A piece of paper could have the appearance of a dollar bill but be counterfeit. It could even be a cheap copy that would fool very few people. To be a dollar bill, a piece of paper must (a) come from an appropriate source (the Federal Government), (b) function in a certain way in an economy (being used for buying and selling), and (c) be identifiable by most people involved in the economy. So, there is a clear difference between the standards by which we typically try to identify dollar bills and the definition of what it is to be a dollar bill. There is likewise an important distinction between the standards by which we typically try to identify true statements and the definition of what it is for a statement to be true.

Relativists about truth, as we said, might be collapsing the distinction between defining conditions and conditions for identification. Two people in different situations can use the same standards, or methods, for discerning the truth and get different results concerning the same statement. One of them can identify the statement as true while the other identifies the same statement as false. Their different determinations can be accounted for in terms of their different situations (including differences in available evidence). If the standards that these two people used in identifying what is true also serve as conditions definitive of what *is* true, then we reach the relativist's conclusion. In that case, the statement under consideration not only is *identified as true* by the first person, but also *is true* for that person, because the truth-defining and truth-identifying criteria are the same for statements. We apparently should admit the possibility of differences between people in their determinations of what is true, even if they are using the same standards for identifying what is true. If there is thus a certain relativity in people's determinations of what is true, and the rules for how properly to determine what is true also are the standards for what is true, it follows that there is relativity about what is true.

We have little, if any, reason to collapse the distinction between the standards for discerning what statements are true and the defining standards for what it is for a statement to be true. The distinction is clearly intelligible and potentially very useful. It is akin to the distinction between how things seem to one (identifying standards for truth) and how they in fact are (defining standards for truth). We must try our best to discern truth from falsehood based on how things appear to us (our identifying standards), but appearances can be misleading, in which case how things really are will differ from how they appear to us. In other words, we can be mistaken in what we believe.

The distinction we have been discussing is necessary for the possibility that we can be *mistaken* in some of our judgments. Without this distinction, we could never be mistaken, as long as we correctly apply an acceptable set of standards for discerning the truth. The rules we follow for finding the truth would constitute the truth itself. Since it seems clearly wrong to deny the possibility of being mistaken in this way, we should preserve the distinction we have been discussing, and if we preserve the distinction between criteria for discerning the truth and defining criteria for being true, then we eliminate the foregoing argument for relativism about truth.

Relativists about truth must face a serious dilemma arising from this simple question: Is the supposed truth of relativism (about truth) *itself* relative? That is, is it relative to the mere beliefs of some individual or group of individuals? If, on the one hand, it is relative in that way, then the supposed truth of relativism would seem not to differ at all from the mere *opinion* of some individual or group of individuals. If, on the other hand, the truth of relativism is not relative in that way, then we have a supposed truth (namely, the truth of relativism) that is incompatible with the relativist claim that all truth is relative to individuals or groups of individuals. On either alternative of this dilemma, relativism about truth is in deep trouble.

Relativists about truth might rely on some arguments different from those we have considered. They might, for instance, preserve the distinction between our standards for discerning the truth and the definition of truth yet still claim that the definition of what it is for a statement to be true depends in some way on facts relative to particular knowers. To explore this possibility further, we should examine some of the competing philosophical theories about what truth is. The remainder of this chapter is concerned with finding the defining criteria for truth. We will not be concerned with the criteria for how we may discern the truth, as the latter topic will emerge in Chapter 5.

TRUTH AND CORRESPONDENCE

According to a longstanding tradition about what it is for a statement to be true, there must be some appropriate *correspondence* between true statements and actual features of the world. For instance, the true statement that you are reading this book corresponds, in some sense, to the actual features of the world in your immediate environment. Versions of this idea appear in the writings of many philosophers throughout the history of Western philosophy.

True statements correspond, in some sense, with reality, and false statements fail to correspond to how things actually are in the world. The idea is intuitively clear at least at the outset. For example, the statement that Chicago is a large American city is true, it seems, because it corresponds to the fact that Chicago *is* a large American city. The statement that Seattle is south of Los Angeles is false, it seems, because it fails to correspond to the facts. Specifically, it is at odds with the fact that Seattle is *north* of Los Angeles. If we employ this correspondence definition of truth, we will not be relativists about truth. The truth, on this view, is not relative to particular people. Rather, it arises from how things are in the world, perhaps altogether independently of human beliefs. As Chapter 3 suggested, a statement may be "approximately" true, and a correspondence definition of truth must have the resources to accommodate this fact. In the case of approximately true belief, the relation between our mental representation of the world and the world itself may be more or less accurate.

The correspondence definition of truth has its roots in Aristotle's claim, in Book IV of the *Metaphysics*, that a statement is true if and only if it either says of what is *that* it is or says of what is not *that* it is not. A statement is false, on this view, if and only if it either says of what is *that* it is not or says of what is not *that* it is.

This wording may be somewhat perplexing at first, but the key idea is crystal clear on reflection. The statement that Chicago is a large American city is true because it says of what is (Chicago's being a large American city) *that* it is (that Chicago is a large American city). The statement that Seattle is south of Los Angeles is false because it says of what is not (Seattle's being south of L.A.) *that* it is (that Seattle is south of L.A.).

Despite its intuitive appeal, the correspondence definition of truth faces some difficulties. The first problem is that it is difficult to spell out exactly what the relation of *correspondence* between a statement (or belief) and the world amounts to. One proposal asserts that correspondence amounts to a kind of *picturing* relation. True statements, on this view, accurately picture how things are. This interpretation is somewhat plausible at least for statements that describe directly some state of affairs, such as the location of some object. "The desk is next to the window" seems to picture through the use of names and grammatical relations the physical situation in which the desk is spatially next to the window.

Talk of a picturing relationship falls short when applied to many cases. Consider statements about what *would* happen in some counterfactual (that is, not actual) situation. "If you were President of the United States, you would be famous" is a true statement, but it is difficult to see what reality it *pictures*. In fact, it is difficult to identify any reality to which it *corresponds*. There are also true statements about what *should* be the case, in contrast to what *is* the case. These are called *normative statements*. For example, "You should help someone whose life is threatened if you are able and if doing so does not threaten your own life" seems to be a true statement. Again, it is hard to see what reality this pictures, or what reality this corresponds to. Many of our more complex true statements seem not to correspond (directly, at least) to any aspect of the world.

We might be able to avoid problems with the notion of correspondence if we formulate a definition of truth that does not rely on any such specific concept. We could define a true statement more simply as any statement such that what it asserts to be the case is in fact the case. Our previous counterfactual claim is clearly true, because what it asserts to be the case is the case, specifically that if you were the President, you would be famous. Our normative claims can likewise be true in a simple way if what they assert to be the case is the case. This simpler version of the correspondence definition of truth, which avoids any specific notion of correspondence, resembles Aristotle's claim that it is true, for example, to say of what is (the case) that it is (the case).

Alfred Tarski's recent influential "semantic approach" to truth is, according to some philosophers, a correspondence approach to truth. Tarski introduced the following principle not as a definition of truth but as an adequacy condition that must be met by any acceptable definition of truth: X is true if and only if P (where "P" stands for a declarative sentence, and "X" stands for the name of that sentence). Given Tarski's condition, the sentence "All surgeons are wealthy" is true if and only if all surgeons are wealthy. Because what follows "if and only if" in Tarski's adequacy condition picks out an actual situation to which the relevant true sentence is appropriately related, various philosophers have regarded Tarski's condition as specifying a correspondence requirement on truth. Philosophers still disagree, however, over whether Tarski offers a correspondence approach to truth.

An apparent epistemological problem confronts any definition that characterizes truth as a relation between a statement (or belief) on the one hand and the world on the other. The problem is that we seem not to be in a position to judge, in a noncircular manner, whether the statement is related in the appropriate way to the world. Confirming any such judgment about appropriate relation, without circularity, apparently requires that we have some (cognitive) access to the world itself that is not mediated by our acceptance of a statement about the world or by other processes subject to skeptical challenge. It *might* be the case that we cannot have such (cognitive) access that is not mediated by such processes. This is a controversial matter among philosophers.

If we lacked the kind of access required, we would then not be in a position to make, without circularity, the required comparison between a statement and the aspect of the world it is about. Chapter 8 will return to a version of this epistemological problem.

If this is a genuine problem, it is only a challenge concerning how we identify what statements are true. It does not challenge a correspondence definition of truth, because a statement can be in the appropriate (truth) relation to the world even though we are not in a position to discover this relation. We may face a challenge here regarding our finding the correct standards for discerning the truth, but this is not a problem for the definition of truth as some sort of correspondence relation between a statement and the world.

We can illustrate that truth as correspondence may not depend on our knowledge of truth or our ability to discern truth. Consider the view that the relevant truth relation may be causal in a special way. According to this view, the key relation between a true statement and the world is causal, and perhaps can be understood by comparison with the relation between a proper name and the thing it names. Use of the name "Elvis Presley" is reference fixing, as some philosophers say. Occurrences of this name pick out the object, Elvis, and in so doing, relate the name causally to the world. This picking-out relation is complex, presumably including initial events such as naming the child, and later social processes by which these uses of the name "Elvis Presley" co-varied with his changing features, such as sideburns and weight. Because this co-variation seems not to be accidental, many philosophers regard it as reflecting some kind of causal relation.

The truth of the claim "Elvis Presley liked greasy late-night snacks" is determined in part by the fact that "Elvis Presley" refers to the person it does. If we substitute a different name, for instance "Shirley Temple," then the truth value of the resulting statement may switch from true to false. So, it seems that the truth relation depends in some way on the reference relation. If the reference relation is causal, then the truth relation depends on a causal relation, even if it is not identical with one. Since the relevant causal relation can obtain without our knowing it, truth will be correspondingly knowledge independent.

It should be no surprise that some truth is independent of our knowledge. After all, if there is a mind-independent world, and our knowledge is limited, then truth can naturally outstrip what we know. For example, there seem to be many truths about Pluto, Jupiter, and Mars beyond our knowledge, perhaps awaiting our discovery.

TRUTH AND COHERENCE

The general difficulties surrounding the task of specifying exactly what type of relation is required between a statement and the world have led some philosophers to develop a significantly different definition of truth. They have defined truth in terms of a relation between statements. The *coherence* definition of truth claims that a statement is true if and only if it stands in an appropriate relation to some system of other statements. The appropriate relation is called *coherence*. This definition of truth was presented by Spinoza (1632–1677) and Hegel (1770–1831), and more recently it is commonly associated with Brand Blanshard.

One important matter the coherence view must address is the nature of coherence. What is it for a statement to "cohere" with some system of other statements? One possibility appeals to the notion of logical implication, stating that a statement coheres with a system of other statements if and only if it follows logically from that system of statements or logically implies some subset of that system. Coherentists about truth sometimes propose the system of mathematical truths as a paradigm of a coherent system yielding truth. It is less than obvious, however, what kind of actual system will serve as a coherence basis for all truths.

A problem of circularity arises if we define "truth" in terms of coherence, and then define "coherence" in such a way that the relevant notion of truth is presupposed. Coherentists about truth might define "coherence" by means of a list of formal inferences, that is, grammatically defined forms of inference (such as "If P then Q, and P; therefore, Q") that do not presuppose the notion of truth in question. We shall then need to know, however, why we should accept those formal inferences as definitive of truth rather than some others, including conflicting inferences. One might argue that a coherentist about truth cannot justify a list of inference forms without relying on a notion of implication that presupposes the very notion of truth in need of definition. Whatever the fate of this problem, the trademark of coherentism about truth is that it does not define "truth" in terms of a special relation between statements and the nonpropositional world, but rather in terms of systematic interconnectedness of statements.

The relation of coherence is difficult to specify in a way that yields a plausible coherence definition of truth. It is often left at an intuitive level of explanation. The main problem, however, concerns what system of statements a statement must cohere with to be true. It might be the entire system of some person's beliefs, or it might be a system of beliefs common to some culture, or it might be some system of statements not directly related to any person's beliefs. This matter, we shall see, resists easy resolution in favor of a coherence definition of truth.

Consideration of what system a statement must cohere with to be true makes it clear that the coherence definition of truth could be a relativist view of truth in the sense that statements are true relative to some system of statements. If the relevant system comes from some individual's set of beliefs, then truth will be relative to individuals. Different people with different systems of background beliefs will have different statements cohering with their personal systems and will consequently have different, perhaps even conflicting, statements be true. A statement can cohere with one person's system of beliefs, and hence be true relative to that system, while failing to cohere with some other person's system of beliefs, hence being false relative to that system. People who find this dramatic relativization of truth unacceptable will be inclined to reject such a version of coherentism about truth. Indeed, one might take the relativization of truth to individuals as a *reductio ad absurdum* of any such version of coherentism.

We should consider the possibility of a delusional person who has a system of beliefs that is mostly false. It seems obviously wrong to claim that a statement counts as true just because it coheres with such a delusional individual's system of beliefs. Our common sense tells us that such coherence might even be closer to a definition of falsehood. Of course, our common sense might be unreliable here, having been shaped too much by some version of the correspondence theory of truth. Even so, the possibility that an individual's belief system is overwhelmingly false apparently yields a good reason to deny that coherence with an individual's beliefs is constitutive of truth.

Similar difficulties carry over to a coherentist's appeal to some system of beliefs common to a particular culture. This view would relativize truth to cultures. We should note, in keeping with the previous objection, that it is possible for a system of beliefs common to a particular culture to be largely false. Some people might even level this sort of criticism against their own culture, if they have evidence that their culture is largely mistaken. Endorsement of the possibility of widespread error might result from prior acceptance of some version of the correspondence definition of truth. Even so, anyone who rejects the relativization of truth to particular cultures will be inclined likewise to reject the cultural version of the coherence definition of truth.

A supposedly truth-making system of statements might be independent of any individual or culture. It is, however, difficult to specify what that system of statements should be. Coherentists cannot stipulate that it be some appropriate set of *true* statements, because they aim to supply a definition of truth. A system of statements that is merely *consistent* will not do, because it is possible to have two different self-consistent systems of statements that are incompatible with each other. Given a coherence approach, there will be nothing that distinguishes one of these systems as the truth-making coherent system and the other as false owing to its failure to cohere with the previous system. Any version of the coherence definition of truth must specify the defining conditions for the truth-making coherent system of statements. Without such a specification, we may plausibly refrain from accepting the coherence definition of truth.

The emphasis on coherence, however coherence is finally specified, seems more obviously relevant to matters of epistemic justification than to matters of truth. Chapter 5 will discuss coherence in the context of theories of justification. For now, however, we should avoid confusing coherence as a definition of truth and coherence as a guideline for discerning, or identifying, truth.

TRUTH AND PRAGMATIC VALUE

The American pragmatists William James (1842–1910) and John Dewey (1859–1952) defended pragmatism regarding the definition of truth. The *pragmatic* definition of truth asserts that a statement is true if and only if it is *useful* in a certain way. The specific kind of usefulness relevant here is, on the most charitable interpretation, *cognitive* usefulness for unifying our experience of the world; it is not usefulness in the general everyday sense. Pragmatists emphasize that truth is a certain kind of validation or verification that ideas receive when they are put to use in our interacting with the world.

The pragmatic definition of truth is relativist, because the relevant kind of usefulness definitive of truth can vary from person to person and from culture to culture. If a particular belief proves useful for one person but not useful for another person, then it is true relative to the first person but false relative to the second person. One person may find it useful — even cognitively useful relative to background beliefs — to believe that his psychological attitudes determine his physical condition; another person may not find this useful to believe. Given pragmatism, truth will vary accordingly. Anyone opposing a defining connection between truth and something as apparently relative and variable as cognitive usefulness will be inclined to reject the pragmatic theory of truth.

Pragmatists have not said enough about the exact nature of the kind of *usefulness* they claim to be definitive of truth. On some pragmatic accounts, the notion of truth seems to be just the notion of epistemic warrant, or justification. One can admit the importance of considerations of cognitive usefulness for the *justification* of a belief but still deny that such usefulness is definitive of *truth*. Collapsing the distinction between conditions of truth and conditions of justification eliminates, quite implausibly, the possibility of justified false beliefs. It seems that on any specific notion of usefulness that pragmatists have offered, it is possible for a belief to qualify as useful but still be false. Some false beliefs can, of course, prove to be cognitively useful. Pragmatists, however, may have strong intuitions that a statement *cannot* be cognitively useful and still fail to be true. Chapter 9 will explain how one may adjudicate such conflicts between intuitions about basic philosophical concepts.

KINDS AND NOTIONS OF TRUTH

Chapter 1 introduced some important distinctions between different kinds of truth. Aristotle introduced the distinction between necessary truth and contingent truth. A statement is necessarily true if and only if there is no possibility that it is false. Statements in mathematics, such as "2 + 2 = 4," seem necessarily true if they are true at all. "2 + 2 = 4" is not *just* true; it cannot be false. Contingent truths are truths that could have been false. "Washington D.C. is the capital of the United States" is true, but it could easily have been false and was false at one time. It is not necessarily true.

Chapter 1 introduced a distinction between analytic and synthetic statements. A true analytic statement is a statement true simply in virtue of the definitions of the terms it contains. "All bachelors are unmarried" is a standard example of an analytic truth, because a bachelor is unmarried *by definition*. Earlier we used the example of "All stop signs indicate that one should stop" as an analytic truth, because a stop sign by definition is a sign that indicates a stop. By contrast, "Some bachelors are named Bubba" is a contingent truth, because there is nothing in the definition of "bachelor" requiring that some bachelors be named Bubba. Earlier we used "All stop signs are red" as an example of a contingent truth, because there is nothing in the definition of a stop sign requiring that all stop signs be red.

The analytic-synthetic distinction has been disputed among contemporary philosophers since 1951, when W. V. Quine published his famous challenge to the distinction, in his "Two Dogmas of Empiricism" (1951). Quine's challenge is based on arguments showing that none of the prominent accounts of analyticity (up to 1951) is ultimately satisfactory, owing to what Quine regards as their unacceptable obscurity or circularity. Since 1951 there have been numerous attempts to undercut Quine's challenge. Some of these attempts seek to give clear noncircular criteria for a proposition's being analytically true, while others question the need for such clear criteria.

A philosopher *might* be a pluralist about the nature of truth, offering different analyses and criteria for different kinds of truth. For instance, one might be a correspondence theorist concerning observational synthetic truths and a coherence theorist (or, alternatively, a pragmatist) concerning theoretical synthetic truths and analytic truths. Such a pluralistic approach would require a precise explanation of the combined theories, and its philosophical attractiveness would depend on its success in answering the questions we have raised in this chapter.

Our survey of various approaches to truth may suggest a general lesson. Even if philosophers can agree on some general, rather vague notion of truth, some philosophers evidently use different specific concepts of truth: for example, correspondence, coherentist, and pragmatist concepts. This empirical lesson indicates divergence in specific notions of truth in circulation. Such divergence counts against potentially uncritical talk of "the" notion of truth, at least if a specific notion is at issue. This does not, however, entail substantive relativism implying that whatever a person or a group believes is automatically true; it allows for nonrelativist notions of truth. Variability in notions of truth does not make mere (shared) belief a sufficient condition of actual truth. In particular, this divergence in notions of truth does not require an "anything goes" attitude toward truth.

We have seen the importance of distinguishing defining criteria for truth and criteria for epistemic justification. It is important to keep the notions of truth and justification distinct to allow for the possibility of justified false belief (and unjustified true belief). We are sometimes justified in believing statements that are nonetheless false. This intuition could be wrong, but it is one of the firmest common-sense intuitions we find in epistemology; so we should ask whether there is a sound basis for preserving it.

In sum, then, we have found good reasons for keeping distinct the defining standards for truth and the identifying standards for truth, the latter being more appropriate to epistemic justification. As a result, we have expressed doubts about relativism concerning truth. Beliefs, of course, may be relative to individuals and cultures, but it does not follow, of course, that truth itself is similarly relative. If our quest for truth is indeed a quest for objectivity, as many philosophers have held, then something like a correspondence notion of truth captures the desired objectivity better than coherentism and pragmatism about truth. Perhaps, then, Aristotle was on the right track so very long ago. We have just considered accounts of truth and belief. We turn now to the third essential condition of the tripartite analysis of knowledge: epistemic justification.

5

Justification and Beyond

Justification, Truth, and Defeat

Our knowing that it will snow in Chicago next winter does not rest on lucky guesswork. Mere lucky guesswork does not yield genuine knowledge, although it can make for a good day at the race track. Even if your groundless guess at the race track is true and confidently believed by you, it still is not knowledge. You do not thereby *know* that your chosen horse is a winner.

Genuine knowledge requires not only truth and belief, but also that the satisfaction of the belief condition be appropriately related to the satisfaction of the truth condition. That is, on the traditional approach, genuine knowledge requires that a knower have an "adequate indication" that a believed proposition is true. This amounts to the requirement that true beliefs qualifying as knowledge must be justified. So, on the traditional view, knowledge has a justification condition. The required "adequate indication" of truth, according to Plato, Kant, and many other philosophers, is *evidence* indicating that a proposition is true. These philosophers thus hold that knowledge must be based on evidence, or justifying reasons. The kind of justification crucial to knowledge is called *epistemic* justification.

Even if knowledge requires justification, a justified belief can be false. (We are now excluding necessary truths — such as those of logic and mathematics — and focusing on contingent truths.) In allowing for justified false beliefs, contemporary epistemologists endorse *fallibilism* about justification. Fallibilism acknowledges that a proposition can enjoy overwhelming evidence or justification but still be false. Recall that the Ptolemaic astronomers before Copernicus were, according to most philosophers, justified in holding their geocentric model of the universe even though it was false. The way the world actually is need not, for better or worse, agree with what our best evidence indicates.

We may distinguish between *deductive* and *inductive* justification. When a justifying proposition logically entails what it justifies, deductive justification obtains. For instance, the propositions *that all philosophers are argumentative* and *that Bertrand Russell is a philosopher* entail, and thus can deliver deductive justification for, the belief that Bertrand Russell is argumentative. The former supporting propositions logically guarantee that the belief about Russell is true. That is, it is logically impossible for those supporting propositions to be true while the belief about Russell is false.

Justification for a proposition, according to contemporary epistemologists, need not logically entail the proposition justified. In other words, it is not the case that necessarily if the justifying proposition is true, then the justified proposition is true too. Inductive justification obtains when a justifying proposition does not logically entail what it justifies. More specifically, it obtains when if the justifying proposition is true, then the justified proposition is, to some extent, *probably* true. Consider, for example, the propositions *that almost all contemporary philosophers have taken a logic course* and *that the authors of this book are contemporary philosophers.* These propositions can yield inductive justification for the belief that the authors of this book have taken a logic course. As it happens, the latter belief is true, but its truth is not required for its being inductively justified by the propositions in question.

(Truth is not a necessary condition for a justified proposition.) Contemporary epistemologists do not share a uniform account of the sort of probability central to inductive justification, but this need not detain us.

Epistemic justification is, according to most contemporary epistemologists, *defeasible*, that is, subject to defeat. A justifying proposition, in other words, can cease to be justifying for you when you acquire additional justification beyond your current evidence. For instance, your justification for believing that there is a pool of water ahead on the highway can be defeated by new evidence acquired from approaching (and seeing the dryness of) the relevant spot on the road. Another case of defeated justification occurs when you see an apparently red table across the room but come to acquire, after closer examination, good evidence that a red light is shining on the table. You thereby lose your initial justification for thinking that the table itself is red. Justification is thus subject to change with the acquisition of new evidence. In this respect, justification differs from truth, which does not change with changes in evidence. Your *beliefs* about what is true may change with changing evidence, but it does not follow that the truth concerning what you believe itself changes too.

INFERENTIAL JUSTIFICATION AND THE REGRESS PROBLEM

Many philosophers have investigated the kind of justification we have for our beliefs about the external world, including familiar beliefs implying the existence of household physical objects. Most contemporary epistemologists hold that such beliefs are justified inductively, in terms of justification that does not logically entail (or, logically guarantee the truth of) the beliefs justified. Some skeptics have demanded stronger, deductive support for beliefs implying that external (that is, mind-independent) objects exist, on the ground that inductive support can lead us into error too easily. Other skeptics have questioned whether we can have even inductive, probabilistic justification for beliefs implying that external objects exist. They worry that we lack an adequate base for ascribing high probability to our familiar beliefs about mind-independent objects.

The Regress Problem

Some skeptics have used a *regress argument* to contend that we are not justified in believing any proposition implying the existence of the external world. Their regress argument raises the question whether, and if so how, we are justified in holding any belief about the external world on the basis of other beliefs, that is, by means of *inferential justification*. Skeptical use of the regress argument aims to establish that each of the available accounts of inferential justification fails, and that inferential justification is not possessed by us, or at least that we cannot reasonably claim to have such justification.

The fundamental skeptical worry underlying the regress argument is this: If one's belief that external objects exist is supposedly justified on the basis of another belief, how is the latter, allegedly justifying belief itself justified? Is it supposedly justified by some other belief? If so, how is the latter belief itself justified? This troublesome line of questioning can continue indefinitely. Suppose you believe, for example, that Toyotas are reliable cars on the basis of your belief that *Consumer Reports* magazine has reported that they are reliable. Skeptics will question the justification of not only the latter belief but also the underlying belief that *Consumer Reports* is trustworthy in its assessment of the reliability of Toyotas. Each of your supporting beliefs will be open to skeptical questioning about its justification.

We seem threatened by an endless regress of required justifying beliefs. Such a regress, in any case, seems too complex to support, or otherwise figure in, our actual everyday reasoning. Our options, in general, are as follows: either (i) explain why an endless regress of required justifying beliefs is not actually troublesome; (ii) show how we can stop the threatening regress, thus identifying how it ends; or (iii) accept the skeptical conclusion that inferential justification is impossible, or at least not actually possessed by us.

Consider an illustration of the problem of inferential justification. While walking along Lake Michigan, we decide that sailing would be pleasant but dangerous today. Our belief that sailing is dangerous today is supported by some of our other beliefs. We believe, for example, that (a) weather forecasters have predicted lightning storms in our area today, (b) there are storm clouds overhead, and (c) the forecasters' reports and the presence of the storm clouds are reliable indicators of impending lightning. Our belief that sailing is dangerous today receives support from our belief that $a-c$ are true. What, however, supports $a-c$ for us? Other beliefs of ours will, naturally enough, contribute some support. So, the chain of inferential justification will continue. Support for a might include our belief that (d) we heard radio reports today from some weather forecasters. Support for b might include our belief that (e) we see dark thunderclouds overhead. Our support for d and e might be similarly inferential, thus extending our chain of inferential justification even further.

Apart from skepticism, contemporary epistemologists have offered four general replies to the regress problem.

Epistemic Infinitism

The first reply, called *epistemic infinitism*, states that regresses of inferential justification are infinite, but that this does not undermine genuine justification. According to infinitism, our belief that sailing is dangerous today would be justified by belief a above, belief a would be justified by belief d, belief d would be justified by a further belief, and so on without end. While attracting very few representatives, such infinitism was supported by Charles Peirce (1839–1914), the founder of American pragmatism. Infinitism implies that we must have an infinity of justifying beliefs to have any inferentially justified belief. It implies that endless regresses of supporting beliefs are not a problem for, but are actually crucial to, genuine inferential justification.

Some skeptics have argued that infinite chains of supposed inferential justification do not, and cannot, yield genuine justification. They contend that no matter how far back we go in an endless regress of inferential justification, we find beliefs that are only *conditionally* justified: that is, justified *if*, and *only if*, their supporting beliefs are justified. In the previous example, our belief that sailing is dangerous today is, it seems, only conditionally justified in this respect. This belief of ours about sailing will be justified if and only if its supporting beliefs are justified too. The problem, however, is that the supporting beliefs themselves are at most conditionally justified too. They are justified if, and only if, *their* supporting beliefs are justified. At every point in the endless chain, according to skeptics, we find a belief that is merely conditionally justified, and not actually justified.

Some skeptics will add that our having an infinity of supporting beliefs apparently requires an infinite amount of time, given that belief-formation for each of the supporting beliefs takes a certain amount of time. We humans, for better or worse, do not have an infinite amount of time. Skeptics doubt, therefore, that our actual justification includes infinite regresses of justifying beliefs. Evidently, then, proponents of infinitism have some difficult explaining to do. As a result, infinitism has attracted very few public supporters throughout the history of epistemology. It is, nonetheless, a logically possible approach to the regress problem, at least according to some philosophers.

Epistemic Coherentism

A second, very influential reply to the regress problem is *epistemic coherentism*: the view that all justification is system dependent in virtue of "coherence relations" among beliefs. Justification for any belief, according to such coherentism, ends in a system of beliefs with which the justified belief coheres. Coherentists thus deny that justification is linear in the way suggested by infinitism. They claim that all justification of beliefs depends on coherence within a system of beliefs.

Typically we can trace the specific reasons for our beliefs only through a short line of justifying beliefs, or inferential justification. We quickly arrive at rather general beliefs deeply entrenched in our basic view of the world, a view that seems to be justified largely by the way its constituent beliefs "hang together" as a coherent comprehensive portrait of the world. For example, the earlier belief about the dangerous sailing conditions depends for its support on beliefs about news reports and beliefs about weather conditions. It is often difficult to locate justification for such beliefs in a single justifying proposition. Ordinarily, such beliefs lead rather to a *network* of beliefs about the significance of such phenomena as visual indicators of the weather, normal patterns of weather, and various types of testimony. We evidently rely on broad portraits of how things generally are in order to support claims about specific situations. Similarly, our broad portraits of the world seem justified, not by any single line of justification from one proposition to another, but by global, or systematic, considerations of coherence.

A common inspiration for coherentists is the kind of systematic, or holistic, justification offered by the sciences. Physics, chemistry, biology, and so on apparently offer a wide-ranging system of beliefs on the basis of which other beliefs can be justified via coherence — via their fitting into the system in an identifiable manner. The wide-ranging views of the sciences "hang together" in a way that offers an ideal for other justified beliefs. The relevant ideal, according to coherentists, is the basis of justification in a systematic network of beliefs.

A coherence theory of *epistemic justification*—so-called *epistemic coherentism* — differs from a coherence theory of *truth*. A coherence theory of truth, of the sort endorsed by Brand Blanshard (1939; 1980) and various other philosophers, aims to specify the meaning of "truth" or the essential nature of truth. A coherence theory of justification, in contrast, aims to explain the nature not of truth, but of the kind of justification essential to knowledge. Recent proponents of epistemic coherentism, of one version or another, include: Sellars 1975; Rescher 1979; Harman 1986; Lehrer 1990; and BonJour 1985. Some historians of philosophy regard Spinoza and Hegel as proponents of epistemic coherentism.

Epistemic coherentists have confronted two important questions: First, what kind of coherence relation is essential to justified belief? Second, what kind of belief system must a justified belief cohere with? Regarding the first question, many epistemic coherentists acknowledge *logical-entailment* relations and *explanatory* relations as coherence relations among beliefs. We have already identified the nature of logical entailment: One belief logically entails another if the truth of the first guarantees the truth of the second. Explanatory coherence relations obtain when some of our beliefs effectively explain why some other of our beliefs are true. For example, your belief that it is snowing outside might, in conjunction with various background beliefs, effectively explain the truth of your belief that the dining-room windows are all white. In that case, the beliefs in question would cohere. Another example of explanatory coherence, from sociology: The generalization that humans tend to derogate "out-groups," or groups to which they themselves do not belong, partly explains personal beliefs that incline toward racist attitudes. We should, however, understand explanatory coherence in a way that allows for explanatory relations between beliefs that are actually false, since epistemically justified beliefs can be false.

Regarding the second question, not just any coherent belief system will confer the kind of justification relevant to epistemic coherentism. Some coherent belief systems, including those consisting just of science-fiction propositions, are obviously false and thus unable to offer a basis for epistemically justified belief. Nobody would claim, for example, that the elaborate story line of *Star Trek* (or, for those innocent of TV, the *Urantia Book*) delivers, as a result of its remarkable coherence, justified beliefs about the real world. (Note, however, that mere falsity does not preclude epistemic justification.) The availability of coherent systems of science-fiction propositions illustrates that epistemic justification is not conferred just by coherence in a belief system. The kind of coherent belief system that confers epistemic justification must be special in some way. We cannot easily specify, however, what exactly this special feature is, and coherentists, in any case, have not reached agreement on what it is. Some have suggested that our coherent belief-system must, to confer empirical epistemic justification, stand in appropriate causal relations to our perceptual, cognitive, and social environment. Still, the appropriate causal relations resist easy specification, especially if we aim to allow for justified false belief.

Epistemic coherentism implies that the justification of any belief depends on that belief's coherence relations with other beliefs. Such coherentism is thus system oriented, emphasizing the role of interconnectedness of beliefs in epistemic justification. Skeptics will doubtless ask why we should regard coherence among one's empirical beliefs as a *reliable* indication of empirical truth, of how things actually are in the empirical world. Recall the *Star Trek* example. (We will return to the matter of skepticism in Chapter 8.)

Consider the following *isolation objection* to epistemic coherentism: Epistemic coherentism implies that one can be epistemically justified in accepting a contingent empirical proposition that is incompatible with, or at least improbable given, one's total empirical evidence, particularly one's evidence from perceptual experience. Proponents of this objection do not restrict empirical evidence to empirical propositions believed or accepted. They allow for empirical evidence consisting of nonbelief perceptual experiences. The latter experiences are sensation experiences, and not cognitive in the way beliefs are. For example, you may have a sensation (or, an early-stage perceptual experience) of burnt sienna prior to forming any *belief* about burnt sienna. So, if such sensations are part of your evidence base for empirical justification, it follows that beliefs do not exhaust your evidence base. This objection requires that sensations, and thus empirical input, be a part of one's empirical evidence. It also assumes that your experience of burnt sienna is not identical with your belief that you are experiencing burnt sienna. (On the distinction between sensation and belief, see Dretske 1981.)

The isolation objection seems widely applicable to coherence theories of justification so long as our empirical evidence goes beyond the propositions believed or accepted by us. Suppose, naturally enough, that our empirical evidence includes the subjective contents (for example, burnt sienna) of our perceptual states, which are not themselves beliefs. Such contents, being nonpropositional, are not among what we believe or accept; they are thus not judgments, sentences, statements, or claims. We can, of course, believe that we are having a particular visual experience (of burnt sienna), but this does not mean that the experience itself is a proposition we believe. If the contents of our perceptual states are among our empirical evidence, the isolation objection will bear directly on all coherence theories of justification.

Coherence theories, by nature, make epistemic justification depend just on coherence relations among propositions one believes or accepts. They thus neglect, by their very nature, the evidential significance of the contents of nonbelief perceptual states. As suggested previously, some coherentists restrict justification-conferring systems of beliefs to those having a special causal origin, for example, those beliefs arising spontaneously from perceptual experience. Still, coherentists have not yet offered a widely accepted account of the sorts of belief origins special to belief systems conferring empirical justification. Apart from grounding empirical justification in nonbelief factors, coherentism will apparently be threatened by the isolation objection.

Epistemic Foundationalism and Reliabilism

A third reply to the regress problem is *epistemic foundationalism.* Foundationalism about epistemic justification states that such justification has two tiers: Some instances of justification are noninferential, or foundational, whereas all other instances of justification are inferential, or nonfoundational, in that they derive ultimately from foundational justification. A noninferential, or foundational, belief is justified but it is not justified by means of inference from or dependence on other beliefs; it might be justified, for instance, in virtue of its special relation to one's perceptual experience, which is not itself a belief. Your belief that you now apparently see a book is (we presume) not inferred from other beliefs; it may be justified directly by your current visual sensation involving an epistemology textbook. By contrast, your belief that words fill most of the remaining pages of this book might not be justified by your current visual experience. The latter belief is likely justified, if it is at all, by your general background beliefs about the standard ways of printing books. You believe that philosophy textbooks usually have words filling most of their pages, and this belief inferentially supports your further belief that this book has words filling most of the remaining pages. The two-tiered structural view called foundationalism was proposed in Aristotle's *Posterior Analytics* (as a view about knowledge), and it received an extreme formulation in Descartes's *Meditations*. In addition, epistemic foundationalism is represented, in various forms, by the following: Russell 1940; C. I. Lewis 1946; Chisholm 1989; Alston 1989; Pollock 1986; Audi 1993; Foley 1987; and Moser 1989, among many others.

Many foundationalists differ on two noteworthy matters: their explanation of noninferential, foundational justification, and their explanation of how justification can be transmitted from foundational to nonfoundational beliefs. Some epistemologists, following Descartes, have assumed that foundational beliefs must be *certain* (for example, indubitable or infallible). This assumption underlies *radical* foundationalism, which requires that foundational beliefs be certain and that they guarantee the certainty of the nonfoundational beliefs they support. Two points explain why radical foundationalism attracts few contemporary philosophers. First, very few, if any, of our perceptual beliefs are certain, that is, immune to doubt or error. (For an assessment of some prominent views about the certainty of subjective beliefs about sensations, see Meyers 1988; cf. Alston 1989, chaps. 10, 11.) Second, the beliefs that are the most promising candidates for certainty (for example, the belief that I am thinking) are not informative enough to guarantee the certainty of our specific inferential beliefs about the external world (for example, our familiar beliefs of physics, chemistry, and biology). As a result, even *if* some of our beliefs enjoy certainty, they will nonetheless fail to transfer their certainty to our robust common beliefs about the external world. Radical foundationalism, then, attracts hardly any contemporary philosophers.

Contemporary foundationalists typically endorse *modest* foundationalism. This view implies that foundational beliefs need not possess or yield certainty, and need not deductively support justified nonfoundational beliefs. Foundationalists typically characterize a *noninferentially justified, foundational* belief as a belief whose epistemic justification does not derive from other beliefs. They leave open whether the *causal* basis of (the existence of) foundational beliefs includes other beliefs. We thus should avoid a confusion of (a) what a belief's *justification* derives from and (b) what the causal basis of a belief's *existence* is.

Contemporary foundationalists typically hold that foundationalism is an account of a belief's (or a proposition's) *having* justification for a person, not of one's *showing* that a belief (or a proposition) has justification or is true. Our having justification for a belief does not require that we show, or present, that justification to ourselves or others; nor does it require that we know, or even justifiedly believe, that we have this justification. Showing justification requires a level of sophistication beyond that of merely having justification.

Proponents of modest foundationalism have offered three notable approaches to noninferential, foundational justification: (i) self-justification, (ii) justification by nonbelief experiences, and (iii) justification by a reliable source of a belief, a source that is not itself a belief (for example, memory or sensation). Motivated by the regress problem, proponents of self-justification contend that a foundational belief can justify itself, apart from any evidential support from something else. For instance, in our sailing example, the justification of your relevant beliefs might end in such beliefs as that you "seem to see" a weather report before you and that you "seem to hear" thunder in the distance. The latter beliefs are, of course, about your subjective experiences, but some foundationalists regard them as "self-justifying."

Proponents of foundational justification by nonbelief experiences reject literal self-justification. They hold, following C. I. Lewis 1946, that foundational perceptual beliefs can be justified by nonbelief perceptual experiences (for example, your nonbelief experience involving seeming to see a book) that either make true, are best explained by, or otherwise support those foundational beliefs (for instance, the belief that there is, or at least appears to be, a book here). The relevant nonbelief perceptual experiences are

not themselves beliefs, although they can support beliefs, especially beliefs about the experiences themselves. (For an exposition
of Lewis's influential views on the given element in experience,
see Firth 1969.)

Proponents of foundational justification by reliable origins
hold that noninferential justification depends on belief-forming
sources (for example, perception, memory, introspection) that
are, although not themselves beliefs, *truth conducive* to some
extent in virtue of tending to cause true rather than false beliefs.
Perception is a source of beliefs, and if it yields more true than
false beliefs, it may be able to confer justification, in virtue of its
reliability, on the beliefs it causes and sustains. The view that reliable belief-forming processes confer epistemic justification is
called *epistemic reliabilism*. Epistemic reliabilism of one sort or
another has been defended by Goldman 1986; Alston 1989; and
Sosa 1991, among others.

Reliabilism about foundational justification invokes the *reliabil-*
ity, or truth conduciveness, of a belief's source, whereas the previous nonreliabilist view invokes the particular perceptual
experiences that underlie a foundational belief. The nonreliabilist view, in sharp contrast with reliabilism, allows that perceptual experience could justify a belief even if perception turned
out (unknown to us, of course) to be unreliable. For example, it
may turn out that our perceptual faculties actually distort our
perceptual input in a way that makes perception unreliable. Reliabilism requires that the sources of belief conferring justification
be truth conducive; so if perception is unreliable, it will not justify the beliefs it causes. Many reliabilists divide over what exact
kind or *degree* of truth conduciveness confers epistemic justification, but they all treat reliability as necessary for belief sources
yielding justified beliefs.

Some reliabilists endorse a version of the moderate naturalism
about epistemology introduced in Chapter 2. They thus regard
epistemology as largely (if not exclusively) empirical, and look to
empirical psychology for a characterization of how our belief-forming processes function. Chapter 3 suggested that some components of belief-formation operate beneath the level of conscious

scrutiny. A belief, accordingly, can be formed and sustained by a reliable process even though the believer is unable to state the causal factors that confer reliability and justification on that belief. Reliabilism thus fits well with the kind of epistemic externalism to be identified later in this chapter, which allows for justifying factors inaccessible to a believer.

The actual reliability of a belief-forming process, such as visual perception, does not rule out the *possibility* of error in beliefs based on that process. For example, you might have a visual illusion of water on the road ahead, and thus have a false belief that there is water on the road ahead, even if your visual functioning is generally a reliable belief-forming process. Many reliabilists thus appeal to the *tendency* a belief-forming process has to yield true rather than false beliefs. A false belief in a particular case does not block a truth-conducive tendency in a belief-forming process. Specifying the *exact circumstances* under which a belief-forming process must be reliable if it is to confer justification poses a difficult problem for reliabilists, the so-called "generality problem" (for relevant discussion see Goldman 1986 and Sosa 1991). Reliabilists aim to avoid both an implausibly narrow specification implying that all true beliefs are reliably formed and an implausibly broad specification implying that belief processes that typically yield false beliefs in the actual world, or in normal situations, are nonetheless reliable (say, under some strange imaginary or counterfactual circumstances). Reliabilists acknowledge that belief-forming processes can be more or less reliable; so the question of whether a process yields justification for a belief may resist easy answers.

Despite the aforementioned disagreements, proponents of modest foundationalism typically agree that noninferential justification can, at least in many cases, be defeated after expansion of one's justified beliefs. The justification for your belief that there is a brown spaniel in the corner, for example, might be undermined, or defeated, by the introduction of new evidence that there is a brown light shining on the spaniel in the corner.

Wilfrid Sellars (1975) and Laurence BonJour (1985) have offered an influential argument against all foundationalist views of noninferential justification. They argue that we cannot be non-inferentially epistemically justified in holding any belief, because we are epistemically justified in holding a belief only if we have good reason to think that the belief is true. Having a good reason to think that a belief is true, according to Sellars and BonJour, is itself a belief. This, they claim, entails that the justification of an alleged foundational belief will actually depend on an argument of the following form:

    a. My foundational belief that P has feature F.
    b. Beliefs having feature F are likely to be true.
    c. Hence, my foundational belief that P is likely to be true.

If the justification of our foundational beliefs depends on such an argument, those beliefs will not really be foundational after all. Their justification will then depend on the justification of other beliefs: the beliefs represented by the premises of the argument just presented. In that case, noninferentially justified, foundational beliefs will be a myth.

    Consider an illustration involving our sailing example, in particular your supposedly foundational belief that you *apparently* hear thunder in the distance. The illustration parallels the previous argument: (a) Your foundational belief that you apparently hear thunder in the distance has the special feature of being a belief just about your subjective experience. (b) Beliefs that are just about subjective experiences are likely to be true. (c) So, your foundational belief that you apparently hear thunder in the distance is likely to be true. If the justification of your belief that you apparently hear thunder in the distance depends on such beliefs as *a–c*, then your belief is not foundational after all. It then depends on coherence relations of a sort to other beliefs.

    Sellars and BonJour must face a problem as a result of their argument. It is too demanding to hold that the justification of your belief that P (for any belief you like) requires your being *justified in believing* premises *a* and *b* of their argument. Given the latter requirement, you will be justified in believing that P only if you are *justified in believing that your belief that P has feature F.* In particular, you will be justified in holding your foundational belief that you apparently hear thunder in the distance only if you are justified in believing that this belief has the special feature of being a belief just about your subjective experience. The latter supporting belief will itself be justified, given the view of Sellars and BonJour, only if it too is supported by justifying premises of an argument. Likewise, those needed justifying premises must themselves be supported by further premises of an argument. Given the requirements in question, we apparently have no nonarbitrary way to avoid the devastating implication that similar requirements apply to each of the ensuing infinity of required justified beliefs. It seems doubtful that we have the required infinity of increasingly complex justified beliefs.

One lesson is that if justificational support for a belief must be somehow accessible, or available, to the believer, that accessibility should not itself be regarded as requiring further justified belief, or further justifying premises of an argument. Otherwise, we face the kind of troublesome regress just indicated. Current debates over *internalism* and *externalism* regarding epistemic justification concern what sort of access, if any, one must have to the support for one's justified beliefs. (For some indication of these elaborate debates, see BonJour 1985, chap. 3; Alston 1989; Audi 1993, chap. 11.) Internalism incorporates an accessibility requirement, of some sort, on what provides justification, whereas externalism does not.

Favoring externalism, some epistemologists hold that justification is crucially, but not necessarily exclusively, a matter of the nature of the world external to the subject. For example, inaccessible causal processes may be constitutive of justified perceptual beliefs. Externalists may thus cite the sort of subdoxastic phenomena discussed in Chapter 3. Such phenomena are primitive intentional states inaccessible to consciousness; they thus lie outside the domain of epistemically relevant phenomena typically invoked by internalists. If inaccessible states, whether inside or outside the subject's skin, play an important role in the ultimate justification of some beliefs, then internalism will neglect certain phenomena having an important epistemic function. Involving many technical distinctions, debates over internalism and externalism are currently unresolved in contemporary epistemology.

Foundationalists must explain, beyond the conditions for non-inferential justification, how justification transfers from foundational beliefs to inferentially justified, nonfoundational beliefs. Proponents of modest foundationalism, unlike radical foundationalists, allow for nondeductive, probabilistic connections that transmit epistemic justification. They have not, however, reached agreement on the exact nature of such connections. Some modest foundationalists hold that a kind of "inference to a best explanation" can account for transmission of justification in many cases. For example, the belief that there is a desk before you can, in certain circumstances, offer a best explanation of various foundational beliefs about your perceptual inputs (such as the belief that there is an apparent desk before you), or at least a best explanation of the perceptual inputs themselves. This, however, is a controversial matter among epistemologists. (For discussion, see Goldman 1988; and Moser 1989.)

A longstanding problem confronts versions of foundationalism that restrict noninferential, or foundational, justification to subjective beliefs about what one *seems* to see, hear, feel, smell, and taste. Those versions must explain how such subjective beliefs can yield justification for beliefs about *mind-independent*, external physical objects. Such subjective beliefs do not logically entail beliefs about physical objects. Because extensive hallucination is always possible, it is also always possible that one's subjective beliefs are true while the relevant beliefs about physical objects are false. This point refutes foundationalists who endorse *linguistic phenomenalism*, the view that statements about physical objects can be translated without loss of meaning into logically equivalent statements solely about subjective states characterized by subjective beliefs. (For discussion of this and other versions of phenomenalism, see Cornman 1975.) Perhaps a foundationalist, following Chisholm 1977 and Cornman 1980, can invoke a set of *nondeductive* relations to explain how subjective beliefs can justify beliefs about physical objects, such as the belief that there is an actual textbook before you. This remains a challenge, however, as no set of such relations has attracted widespread endorsement from contemporary foundationalists. Some versions of foundationalism,

however, allow for the noninferential, or foundational, justification of beliefs about physical objects, and thus avoid the problem at hand.

Epistemic Contextualism

A fourth nonskeptical reply to the regress problem is *epistemic contextualism*. This view has been suggested by Ludwig Wittgenstein (1969) and formulated explicitly by David Annis (1978). Wittgenstein sets forth the heart of contextualism with his claim that "at the foundation of well-founded belief lies belief that is not founded" (1969, para. 253). Construing Wittgenstein as stating that at the foundation of justified beliefs lie beliefs that are unjustified, we arrive at an alternative to infinitism, coherentism, and foundationalism. (The interpretation of Wittgenstein's *On Certainty* is a matter of controversy among philosophers; for one effort at interpretation, see Morawetz 1978.)

According to contextualism, in any context of inquiry, the people involved simply assume (the acceptability of) some propositions as starting points for their inquiry. These "contextually basic" propositions, while themselves lacking evidential support, can support other propositions. The lack of evidential support for contextually basic propositions distinguishes these beliefs from the noninferentially justified, foundational beliefs described in the previous section. Contextualists emphasize that contextually basic propositions can vary from social group to social group and from context to context—for example, from theological inquiry to biological inquiry. Thus, what functions as an *unjustified* justifier in one context need not in another. Justification, according to contextualism, is highly sensitive to social context.

A key problem for contextualism comes from the view that *unjustified* beliefs can yield epistemic justification for other beliefs. If we grant that view, we need to avoid the implausible view that *any* unjustified belief, however obviously false, can yield justification in certain contexts. If *any* unjustified proposition can serve as a justifier, we shall be able to justify *anything* we want—

an intolerable result by virtually any standard. For example, we would then be able to justify obviously false beliefs (such as the belief that water below ground can cause divining rods above ground to move) so long as certain other unjustified beliefs were taken for granted. Even if we do typically take certain things for granted in certain contexts of discussion, this does not support the view that there are unjustified justifiers. Perhaps the things typically taken for granted are actually supportable by good reasons. If they are not, we need some way to distinguish them from unjustified beliefs that cannot transmit justification to other beliefs. The contextualist must explain, then, how an unjustified belief—but not just *any* unjustified belief—can confer inferential justification on other beliefs. Contextualists have not reached agreement on the needed explanation.

In sum, the epistemic regress problem for inferential justification is, like many problems of philosophy, a resilient troublemaker. Infinitism, coherentism, foundationalism, or contextualism may offer a viable solution to the problem, but only after epistemologists resolve the relevant problems we have noted.

SUPPLEMENTING JUSTIFICATION: THE GETTIER PROBLEM

Some recent epistemologists have proposed that we give up the traditional justification condition for knowledge. They recommend, following Alvin Goldman (1967), that we construe the justification condition as a *causal* condition. Roughly, the idea is that you know that P if (a) you believe that P, (b) P is true, and (c) your believing that P is causally produced and sustained by the fact that makes P true. That is, you know a proposition if it is true and you believe it and your belief is *caused* by the fact that makes it true. For example, you know that a book is before you if there is a book before you, you believe that a book is before you, and your belief is caused by the fact that there is a book before you. This is the basis of a *causal theory of knowing*, a theory that admits of different manifestations.

A causal theory of knowing faces serious problems from knowledge of universal propositions. Perhaps we know, for instance, that all can openers are produced by humans, but our believing that this is so seems not to be causally supported by *the fact* that all can openers are humanly produced. It is not clear that the latter fact causally produces *any* beliefs. At a minimum, we need an explanation of how a causal theory can account for knowledge of such universal propositions. Proponents of a causal theory of knowledge will, of course, emphasize that the actual causal sources of our beliefs are typically very complex and identifiable only by reliance on our best empirical psychology.

The analysis of knowledge as justified true belief, however elaborated, faces a challenge that initially gave rise to causal theories of knowledge: *the Gettier problem*. Traditionally, many philosophers assumed that justified true belief is sufficient as well as necessary for knowledge. This is a minority position now, mainly because of the "Gettier counterexamples" to this view. In 1963 Edmund Gettier published an influential challenge to the view that if you have a justified true belief that *P*, then you know that *P*. Here is one of Gettier's counterexamples to this view: Smith is justified in believing the false proposition (say, on the basis of the testimony of a trustworthy friend) that (i) Jones owns a Ford. On the basis of *i*, Smith infers, and thus is justified in believing, that (ii) either Jones owns a Ford or Brown is in Barcelona. As it happens, Brown is in Barcelona, and so *ii* is true. Thus, although Smith is justified in believing the true proposition *ii*, Smith does not know *ii*.

Here is another one of Gettier's influential counterexamples: Smith and Jones have applied for the same job. Smith is justified in believing that (a) Jones will get the job, and that (b) Jones has ten coins in his pocket. On the basis of *a* and *b* Smith infers, and thus is justified in believing, that (c) the person who will get the job has ten coins in his pocket. As it turns out, Smith himself actually gets the job, and he happens to have ten coins in his pocket. So, although Smith is justified in believing the true proposition *c*, Smith does not know that *c*.

Gettier-style counterexamples are cases in which a person has justified true belief that *P* but lacks knowledge that *P*. The Gettier problem is just the problem of finding a modification of, or an alternative to, the standard, justified true belief analysis that avoids difficulties from Gettier-style counterexamples. The controversy over the Gettier problem is highly complex and still unsettled.

Some philosophers have alleged that Gettier-style counterexamples rely on the questionable principle that false propositions can justify one's belief in other propositions. These philosophers would claim that Gettier-style examples do not, contrary to their intention, describe cases of actual justification, and thus that they fail to challenge the traditional analysis of knowledge. Many of the counterexamples obviously do rely on the principle in question. There are, however, examples like Gettier's that do not depend on the questionable principle. Here is one example (based on examples formulated by Keith Lehrer and Richard Feldman):

> Suppose Smith knows the following proposition, M: Jones, whom Smith has always found to be reliable and whom Smith has no reason to distrust now, has told Smith, his office-mate, that P: He, Jones, owns a Ford. Suppose also that Jones has told Smith that P only because of a state of hypnosis Jones is in, and that P is true only because, unknown to himself, Jones has won a Ford in a lottery since entering the state of hypnosis. Suppose further that Smith deduces from M its existential generalization, Q: There is someone, whom Smith has always found to be reliable and whom Smith has no reason to distrust now, who has told Smith, his office-mate, that he owns a Ford. Smith, then, knows that Q, since he has correctly deduced Q from M, which he also knows. Suppose, however, that on the basis of his knowledge that Q, Smith believes that R: Someone in the office owns a Ford. Under these conditions, Smith has justified true belief that R, knows his evidence for R, but does not know that R.

Gettier-style examples of this sort have proven especially difficult for attempts to analyze the concept of propositional knowledge.

The history of attempted solutions to the Gettier problem is complex and open-ended; it has not produced consensus on any solution. Many epistemologists take the lesson of Gettier-style counterexamples to be that propositional knowledge requires a *fourth* condition, beyond the justification, truth, and belief conditions. No specific fourth condition has received overwhelming acceptance by epistemologists, but some proposals have become prominent.

The so-called "defeasibility condition" requires that the justification appropriate to knowledge be "undefeated" in the general sense that some appropriate subjunctive conditional concerning defeaters of justification be true of that justification. For instance, one simple defeasibility fourth condition requires of Smith's knowing that P that there be no true proposition, Q, such that if Q became justified for Smith, P would no longer be justified for Smith. So if Smith genuinely knows, on the basis of his visual perception, that Jeanne removed books from the library, then Smith's coming to believe the true proposition that Jeanne's identical twin, Judy, removed books from the library would not undermine the justification for Smith's belief concerning Jeanne herself. For Smith's belief regarding Jeanne to qualify as genuine knowledge, its justification must not be subject to defeat by Smith's learning about Judy or about anything else.

A different approach to the Gettier problem avoids subjunctive conditionals of the previous sort, and claims that propositional knowledge requires justified true belief that is sustained (that is, not defeated) by the collective totality of actual truths. This approach relies on a fourth condition of evidential truth sustenance. The heart of this solution, characterized roughly, is that propositional knowledge will be sustained — will not be undermined — by all truths taken together. This approach requires a detailed account of when justification is undermined and restored, but we shall not digress to technical details. (For a version of the latter approach, see Pollock 1986.)

The Gettier problem, according to many contemporary epistemologists, is epistemologically important. One branch of epistemology seeks a precise understanding of the nature — for example, the essential components — of propositional knowledge. Our having a precise understanding of propositional knowledge requires our having a Gettier-proof analysis of such knowledge. Epistemologists thus need a defensible solution to the Gettier problem, however complex that solution is. This conclusion is compatible with the view that various epistemologists employ different notions of knowledge at any level of specificity.

In sum, then, we have seen that justification is subject to defeat, or undermining, in a way that truth is not. We have also seen that inferential justification resists easy elucidation and admits of a variety of proposed solutions to the epistemic regress problem: including infinitism, coherentism, foundationalism, and contextualism. Whatever solution one favors, the justification condition for knowledge needs some kind of qualification in light of the Gettier problem. It is still an open question in epistemology what exact qualification is correct. Having completed our survey of the essential conditions of knowledge, we turn now to some of the main sources of knowledge. Our focus shifts, correspondingly, from relatively general conceptual issues in epistemology to more empirical matters pertinent to human knowledge.

6

Sources of Knowledge

This chapter examines the sources of knowledge, particularly the matter of where knowledge comes from. It introduces the traditional sources discussed by rationalists and empiricists, and treats such sources as perception and memory. It then turns to the complex and crucial role of testimony in knowledge. Testimony involves a rich network of social dependence, and thus prompts the question of whether, and if so how, the social character of intellectual activities contributes to knowledge.

RATIONALISM, EMPIRICISM, AND INNATISM

Historically, philosophers have held some combination of two positions: rationalism and empiricism. These positions resist simple characterization, but their extreme, polar features can be expressed broadly as follows: Rationalism states that nonempirical reason is the source of all knowledge, whereas empiricism states that sensory experience is the source of all knowledge. Let's begin by looking at basic positions on each side.

Basic empiricism states that we do not have knowledge of reality through the nonempirical use of reason. It states that we cannot know about the reality or unreality of unicorns, for example, simply by examining the *concept*, or the *idea*, of a unicorn. The same holds true for the question of the reality of, say, elephants; we cannot know whether they are real merely through the non-empirical use of reason. *Basic rationalism*, in contrast, affirms that some such knowledge is available to us. We cannot determine whether *elephants* exist through the nonempirical use of reason, but according to basic rationalism we *can* determine, for example, that every event has a cause. Some (but not all) rationalists would also say that we can prove the existence of God through the nonempirical use of reason. If, in keeping with basic empiricism, we do not have knowledge of reality through the nonempirical use of reason, then we lack knowledge of reality by rational intuition or by innate (inborn, or unlearned) universal principles. Knowledge of reality, according to basic empiricism, derives from sensory experience and the empirical use of reason — and from these alone. Basic empiricism maintains that we do have genuine knowledge, and characteristically it holds that we have knowledge of objective, mind-independent reality as well.

Many empiricists are *concept empiricists*, holding that all concepts are directly or indirectly acquired through sensory experience. All simple concepts and many complex concepts are evidently acquired through direct sensory experience. This includes such concepts as the concepts of blue, bitter, dog, and paper. Concept empiricism implies that such complex concepts as the concepts of planet, car, computer, and farmer, although not themselves directly acquired from experience, consist entirely of parts that are so acquired. Concept empiricism sets no special conditions regarding the nature of concept acquisition through sensory experience. It is rather a general alternative to *concept innatism*, the view that we possess some concepts innately, independently of sensory experience. Concept empiricism and basic empiricism are logically independent positions in that one does not entail, or logically imply, the other.

According to rationalism, some propositions have a privileged epistemological status in virtue of their own nature. Consider the following two propositions:

1. Every event has a cause.
2. Two objects cannot be in exactly the same place at the same time.

Such propositions are, according to rationalists, epistemologically special in that they are both knowable *a priori* and nonanalytic, that is, synthetic. They are arguably knowable *a priori* inasmuch as they are not learned or justified on the basis of experience, in the way empirical generalizations are. They are arguably nonanalytic in that they have descriptive content of a sort foreign to analytic (or, definitional) propositions. (See Chapter 1 on analytic truths.) We need not assume now that the previous propositions *1* and *2* are actually both synthetic and knowable *a priori*. We should consider, nonetheless, how there could be synthetic *a priori* knowledge. The issue is whether we can know synthetic propositions independently of sensory experience.

Rationalists and empiricists have given opposing accounts of the propositions in question. Rationalists emphasize the role of reason, and empiricists emphasize the role of sensory experience. Indeed, empiricists typically deny that there is synthetic *a priori* knowledge, such as knowledge of "Every event has a cause," and attempt to explain away either the appearance that it is synthetic or the appearance that it is *a priori*. Let's characterize the *empirical use of reason* as either (a) processes of thinking about the objects of sensory experience or (b) processes of deductive or inductive reasoning from premises deriving from the former processes of thinking. In contrast, let's characterize the *nonempirical use of reason* as processes of thinking other than the empirical use of reason. An inductive inference based on observation reports is an empirical use of reason, but an awareness just of the relation between certain innate ideas (if there are such ideas) is a nonempirical use of reason.

A prominent form of argument by the rationalist observes that a person appears to know that *P*, but that, for special reasons having to do with the particulars of the case, the person could not have learned (or at any rate, did not learn) that P through sensory experience. An instance of this argumentative strategy occurs in Plato's *Meno*, in an episode involving a slaveboy. Socrates asks a slaveboy to answer a series of questions about the relative proportions of sides of a square. The slaveboy makes use of a picture that Socrates has provided but, because slaves in ancient Athens were not educated as Athenian male citizens were, he would not have acquired his knowledge of the square through the empirical process of formal instruction. Since the slaveboy answers the questions about the square correctly, Socrates and his interlocutors conclude that his knowledge is innate, not empirically learned.

Descartes offered a similar argument concerning our knowledge about a chiliagon, a thousand-sided figure. Descartes argued that various mathematical relationships could be deduced from knowledge of the nature of a chiliagon, yet this deduction could not have proceeded on the basis of the inner (introspective) or the outer senses. Were we to be visually presented with such a figure, the angle at every vertex would be so close to 180 degrees that the overall figure would be virtually indistinguishable from a circle. When we attempt to introspect such a figure, Descartes argues, we are faced with a similar problem. Therefore, our knowledge of a chiliagon's features must be innate, and not learned from inner or outer sense.

The rationalist argument for innate knowledge has a modern incarnation, sometimes called the poverty-of-the-stimulus argument. The latter argument infers the existence of innate knowledge about a specific domain, in virtue of its being the best explanation for our acquisition of a particular competence or skill. The most prominent use of this innatist argument occurs in modern linguistics, owing largely to the work of Noam Chomsky. The young child's first language is seldom explicitly taught; nonetheless, by the age of 4 years the child is already speaking remarkably well. No one has explained to the child the syntactic function of a verb, a passive voice, or a subordinate clause. Still, the child uses them all with considerable skill. When the child does receive feedback from the world, it is sometimes contradictory and often variable across speakers. This could be hopelessly confusing for a young child, were it not for the already rich store of linguistic information that the child possesses — or so rationalists have argued.

Another argument for innatism comes from Jerry Fodor (1975); it concludes that most, if not all, of our concepts are innate. This argument proceeds by claiming that the only model of learning we have involves our projecting hypotheses about the world and then confirming or disconfirming them. To project hypotheses, however, we must formulate them in some vocabulary or other. Preverbal children successfully learn about the world, as do such nonhuman animals as dogs and chimps. Because all of the latter lack a natural language, the vocabulary in which the projected hypotheses are internally formulated is not a natural language. It must be some other language: a language of thought. This language of thought cannot have been learned, for it is a precondition for learning; therefore, at least some of our concepts are innate. This is a version of innatism specifically about concepts, but this concept-innatism can contribute to claims about the existence of *a priori* knowledge and the plausibility of rationalism.

A full discussion of innatism about language would go well beyond the scope of this book. To get a sense of the complexity of the topic, however, consider how one might argue against the strong innatist about language learning. Relevant evidence against the innatist might include examples of children raised in relative isolation, with some exposure to spoken language, but who could not themselves speak any natural language. There are just a handful of such cases on record, and yet none of them could speak in a way that even approached normal fluency.

Apparently, language learners depend on perceptual effects of spoken language at least to the extent that, if the language learner is denied access to normal perceptual effects of spoken language, he or she cannot acquire normal fluency. Evidently, then, the stimulus (in this case, audible and visible speech) is not impoverished relative to the language learner's needs. At the same time, these cases are extremely difficult to interpret. It appears that many competencies related to language use in development also depend on human contact and normal social development. If emotional and cognitive development is related to language development, and the former development is stunted by absence of human contact, then we could plausibly predict a corresponding language deficit.

Recent incarnations of innatist arguments were first aimed primarily at behaviorist philosophers and psychologists. In that connection, a crude, relatively unarticulated notion of innateness was sufficient. After all, behaviorists rejected psychological explanations that made unreduced appeal to such unobservable mental phenomena as beliefs and desires. Arguments on both sides of the innatist dispute are complicated and cannot be cogently assessed by coarse appeal to "common sense." In fact, few participants to this dispute have clearly formulated their favored notion of innatism. What exactly is it for a concept to be innate? What is it for a rule to be innate? Can there be innate knowledge if only rules are innate? Is it possible for the mind to be compartmentalized in such a way that some closely related capacities are innate and others are not? These and related questions are still controversial in philosophical and psychological work on the sources of knowledge.

EMPIRICISM, POSITIVISM, AND UNDERDETERMINATION

Empiricism in the history of epistemology has been represented by such influential figures as John Locke, George Berkeley, and David Hume (1711–1776). The dominant strain of empiricism descends from Hume, who claimed that all of our nontautological knowledge arises from sensory experience. Hume's variety of empiricism was motivated by *semantic* considerations, by considerations about meaning. Hume argued that, unless our nonlogical concepts were grounded in sensation, they would be unintelligible; put semantically, terms expressing those concepts would otherwise be meaningless.

Hume's *Enquiry Concerning Human Understanding* ([1748]) promotes the following antimetaphysical verificationism:

> If we take in our hand any volume, of divinity or school metaphysics, for instance, let us ask, *Does it contain any abstract reasoning concerning quantity or number?* No. *Does it contain any experimental reasoning concerning matter of fact and existence?* No. Commit it then to the flames: for it can contain nothing but sophistry and illusion. (Sec. VII, Pt. III)

It is no mystery, then, why the twentieth-century logical positivists who formed the Vienna Circle claimed Hume as one of their chief philosophical forerunners; they shared Hume's antipathy to metaphysics. In particular, they used modern logic, deriving from Gottlob Frege (1848–1925) and Russell, and various analytical techniques to restrict philosophical pursuits to the advancement of "scientific" knowledge, thereby banishing metaphysical concerns from philosophy. Hume's extreme empiricism had questioned the meaningfulness of concepts lacking a basis in experience. The Vienna Circle likewise doubted the cognitive meaningfulness of metaphysical notions and theses that transcend experience by being immune to empirical tests. The logical positivists' doctrines have had a lasting influence on empiricist epistemology.

In the early 1930s a number of logical positivists endorsed a principle of verification regarding meaning. Acknowledging Wittgenstein's influence, Friedrich Waismann, a member of the Vienna Circle and a prominent interpreter of Wittgenstein, published one of the first endorsements: "If there is no way of telling when a proposition is true, then the proposition has no sense whatever; for the sense of a proposition is its method of verification" (1930, p. 5). We can thus put *the verification principle* succinctly: The meaning of a proposition is its method of verification. In other words, you can understand a statement only by knowing what would possibly show it to be either true or false.

If metaphysical claims about gods, souls, essences, values, and the like lack a method of verification, one can use the verification principle to dispense with those claims as meaningless. The

Vienna Circle did indeed dispense with them as meaningless, not just as unknowable. They construed the needed method of verification as a method of justification, or confirmation, in terms of *observable* events or situations. They thus held that every meaningful claim can be expressed in terms of observational claims: that is, claims susceptible to confirmation or disconfirmation on the basis of observation. Moritz Schlick (1936) specified that the meaning of a claim depends not on its actual verification, but only on the *possibility* of its verification on the basis of experience.

The members of the Vienna Circle divided over the nature of the fundamental observational claims that set the standard for confirmation and meaningfulness. One key issue was whether these observational claims are solely about what is given in subjective private experience, and not about intersubjectively testable claims regarding physical states of affairs. Even so, the main problems facing logical positivism concern the status of the verification principle itself.

One noteworthy problem is that some meaningful claims seem not to admit of a "method of verification." If such "nonverifiable" claims could be meaningful, then they are also potential candidates for *knowledge*. Consider, for example, that claim that an omnipotent being exists: a being sufficiently powerful to accomplish anything that can be coherently described. Presumably, you understand this claim, but you have no method of confirmation or disconfirmation for it. You seemingly understand what, in general, it would be for that claim to be true or false. At least our ordinary notions of meaning and understanding allow for this. You lack, however, any means — including any observational means — of confirming or disconfirming that claim. Indeed, there seems not to be even a possible means available to you for confirming or disconfirming that claim. You lack a *method* of verification, but the claim in question still seems meaningful — at least by ordinary standards. If we weaken conditions for verification, to allow for the desired method, we shall thereby prevent the principle of verification from excluding metaphysical claims as meaningless.

What about the principle of verification itself? Does it itself admit of a method of verification resting on observational evidence? This seems unlikely. Our observational evidence, deriving from sensory experience, fails to yield a straightforward method of verification for the verification principle itself. We have no evidence from psychology, for example, that we are always unable to understand a statement unless we comprehend a clear method of verification of that statement. Perhaps, then, the verification principle is meaningless by its own standard for meaningfulness. Perhaps it cannot be verified by experience.

Whatever internal problems plague the verification principle, the aims of logical positivists were clear enough: Use sensory evidence as the only secure basis for knowledge and even meaning, thus rendering illicit and even meaningless the (metaphysical) reference to a mind-independent reality. Our theoretical beliefs — beliefs about unobservable phenomena — and our observational beliefs are, however, underdetermined by our sensory evidence. That is, our beliefs outstrip our sensory evidence in a way that allows for alternative coherent interpretations of that evidence. For example, on the basis of common highway experience, you may have an observational belief that there is a puddle in the road ahead. Your observational input by itself admits of a number of different supposed sources: for example, the illusion produced by rising heat rather than actual water on the road. Our theoretical beliefs are notoriously underdetermined by sensory evidence. When you heat an enclosed volume of gas and observe the sides of the container bulge, there are various initially consistent stories you could tell about what might have caused your sensory experience to be as it is. Further tests might distinguish among more or less plausible hypotheses about the real causes of your sensory evidence. Initially, however, there are many consistent hypotheses, and even after sustained testing we may not be able to eliminate all but one.

In a tradition of quaint but valuable experimentation we find an example of one such clear worry about underdetermination. William Beaumont studied the effects of the "digestive juices" on food. Using as a subject a soldier who had an open musket wound in his gut, Beaumont introduced into this wound a variety of delectables, including cabbage, beef, bread, and raw salted pork.

Each fixed to a silk string, these pieces of food were retracted after recorded intervals, thus allowing Beaumont to observe the effects of the digestive process on them. Beaumont reported in his log that the cabbage and bread disappeared first, while the meat retained much of its original form for several hours.

Rather than immediately conclude that digestive juices acted more effectively on cabbage than on meat, Beaumont states:

> This experiment cannot be considered a fair test of the powers of the gastric juice. The cabbage, one of the articles which was, in this instance, most speedily dissolved, was cut into small, fibrous pieces, very thin, and necessarily exposed on all its surfaces to the action of the gastric juice. The stale bread was porous, and of course admitted the juice into all its interstices; and probably fell from the string as soon as softened, and before it was completely dissolved. These circumstances will account for the more rapid disappearance of these substances than of the pieces of meat, which were in entire solid pieces when put in. ([1833], "Experiment 1 in the First Series," p. 126)

Beaumont was trying to determine the cause of his observation, including the cabbage's disappearance. He recognized that the disappearance had more than one initially plausible explanation. In light of improved theory, he designed experiments in such a way that they would decide between various hypotheses postulating a (typically unobserved) cause. At the same time, Beaumont was concerned with relatively gross phenomena — phenomena regarding whether gastric juices degenerate some foods faster than others.

The existence of alternative coherent explanations makes clear that we can never completely eliminate underdetermination worries. Still, eliminating underdetermination worries need not concern us unless we attempt to answer skeptics. In the wake of the unsuccessful attack on metaphysics waged by the verification principle, there have been no durable proposals to distinguish between empirically meaningful and empirically meaningless statements. What has emerged instead is a consensus that, contrary to many proponents of the verification principle, statements are typically tested in groups. This kind of modest epistemic holism supplies no specific criterion for an intelligible empirical concept. It is a view about *confirmation* rather than meaning. Even so, one thing is clear: Not every empirical concept owes its intelligibility to its being directly correlated with sensory content.

Intuitions and First-Person Reports

Epistemological arguments often begin with what philosophers call "intuitions" about the nature of knowledge. In the previous section we were drawing on intuitions as well, intuitions about meaningfulness, for example. We may think of intuitions, in this connection, as theoretical hunches of a sort: that is, unrefined, relatively spontaneous beliefs that something is (or is not) the case. Reliance on intuitions is sometimes identified with common sense, a primitive store of beliefs whose truth is thought to be established by casual observation. Contrary to some philosophers, intuition, like common sense, is notoriously theory dependent; what someone finds intuitively plausible typically can be predicted from the background theory he or she holds. Many Ptolemaic thinkers, opposing Copernican astronomers, found the heliocentric view of the solar system intuitively implausible, on the grounds that the earth did not "seem" to be moving and that we would constantly feel a breeze if the heliocentric view were true. In addition, some scientists resisted the classification of mercury as a metal, contending that any substance that acted like mercury intuitively ought to be a liquid.

When intuitive protestations are made without elaboration, they may be effectively treated as personal reports, as just so much interesting autobiography. People advancing intuitions alone are stating, in effect, that they find a view plausible or implausible. First-person reports are an important source of knowledge if the subject matter is the person in question. If, however, the subject matter is impersonal (for example, the nature of the stars or the feeding habits of the short-tailed shrew), a first-person report of an intuition does not meet any significant standard of evidence. Like ordinary language, intuition can be a place to start philosophical inquiry, not a place to decide important theoretical issues. Thus, it is no decisive criticism of a complex theoretical position that it is "counterintuitive."

Intuition, in another sense of the term, is a special faculty of perception. Some epistemologists claim that they have knowledge of moral properties via exercise of a faculty of intuition, a faculty adapted to the detection of moral properties. A plausible reply to such a claim may raise forthright questions about the idiosyncratic operation of this faculty. For example, if many others don't enjoy the same operation of such a faculty, why don't they? We appropriately ask this kind of question when individuals report different experiences through the same perceptual faculties under the same perceptual circumstances. We should likewise expect an explanation of the divergence in reports of the products of intuitive faculties. Perhaps an explanation is forthcoming, but none enjoys consensus in contemporary epistemology.

MEMORY

If our claim to knowledge about some event is challenged, we commonly consult our memory. Indeed, sometimes we have only memory as a basis for a knowledge claim. Memories of childhood experiences, for example, are difficult to confirm in the absence of sibling or parental testimony. Suppose you have a memory that, as a child, you caught a filefish in New Jersey's Barnegat Bay. Filefish are typically found in tropical waters or, at any rate, in warmer waters than those of the New Jersey coast. At the same time, the local nuclear power plant accounted for an unusually warm temperature in Barnegat Bay, allowing the environment to support fish of tropical origin. Suppose that someone challenges your claim that you caught a filefish. How would you reply? You could consult a sibling, but perhaps this would confirm only that you caught an unusual fish in the bay. Memory underwrites much of our supposed knowledge that otherwise would not be underwritten at all.

We can lose knowledge through memory loss. Chapter 3 recounted, for instance, that Mrs. T progressively lost her belief, and thus her knowledge, that McKinley was assassinated. On the positive side, you remember (the use of "remember" here is that of a "success verb," succeeding in what it aims to accomplish), and thus know, the capital of Missouri without having retained any specific evidence for this knowledge claim (for the record, it's Jefferson City). Accordingly, some philosophers have claimed that veridical memory, like veridical perception, depends on a memory's standing in the right *causal* relation to the memory's supposed ground. The task of specifying the "right causal relation" is, however, complex, and we need not digress to it.

Memory seems to have a feature of first-person privilege. Although our first-person memories often contain mistaken propositional information (that is, misinformation about the thing purportedly remembered), we seldom seem mistaken that the apparently remembered event happened *to us.* Undeniably, at times something we thought happened to us in fact happened to a friend or a sibling. Cases of this sort resist a simple uniform explanation. In a similar vein, the difficulty surrounding multiple personality phenomena is often first noticed by us when we hear either a clinical report that "the patient has three personalities" or a first-person report that "I have three personalities." What, then, does "the patient" or "I" refer to? This question raises a worry more closely related to the metaphysical topic of personal identity than to the epistemological issue of the role of memory in knowledge. Still, the two topics are worth mentioning together, because memories always have a subject and an object. There are at least two possible ways, then, that memories can be mistaken: when the subject is incorrectly identified and when the object is misidentified.

Although memory is obviously fallible, we often suppose that remembering is like playing back a videotape, and the preponderance of experimental evidence suggests that this supposition is false. Consider the following test strategy for memory (see Loftus and Ketcham 1994). First, subjects view a particular event. Second, they are given verbal information about the event (either with or without misleading crucial details). Third, they are given a memory test with questions about the crucial details. For instance, in one study, subjects watched a series of slides portraying a car accident. Later, some subjects were given a misleading suggestion about the kind of traffic sign that marked a particular intersection. As part of this design, some subjects saw a stop sign at the intersection but were later misinformed that it was a yield sign. Subjects were then given a two-alternative, forced-choice recognition test. Subjects were instructed to identify which of two slides they saw in the slide show. The test items mostly consisted of an event detail paired with a new distractor, but the "critical" test items were an event detail paired with the corresponding misleading, suggested detail (for example, stop sign vs. yield sign). The effect of the misleading suggestion? On the critical test items, subjects who were given Misleading Postevent Information (MPI) were far less accurate than subjects who were not given MPI.

The foregoing misinformation effect in memory is powerful. It is no mere artifact of laboratory memory research. The misinformation effect is controversial only in the sense that psychologists disagree whether it is caused by the obliteration, or "overwriting," of the correct information originally processed rather than by the MPI impairing people's ability to retrieve the original memory. The important point now is that a systematic account of the contribution of memory to knowledge must take account of such complex theoretical issues in the nature of memory: particularly, the reliability of memory, its vulnerability to suggestion, and the damage that can result from MPI.

THEORETICAL UNIFICATION

Another source of knowledge is available through the evidence of unification of disparate phenomena. The fact that knowledge has distinguishable sources makes possible a certain strategy for justification. On the assumption that any object that is real has many effects (for example, a tree provides cool shade, supplies oxygen, consumes water, etc.), our knowledge concerning an object can stem from various evidential routes. Where the existence or nature of something is controversial or ill-understood, it is evidence for a specific hypothesis about the thing that, if true, the hypothesis would unify a variety of observational and theoretical commitments. Our account of gravity unifies not just diverse orbital systems but also the behavior of individual bodies within those systems. The atomic theory of matter explains how otherwise disparate phenomena, such as Brownian motion, electrolysis, and beta decay, are causally related.

We find the strategy of theoretical unification displayed in early modern experimental science, among other contexts. An example of the guiding principle of explanatory unification occurs in Robert Boyle's *New Experiments Physicomechanical Touching the Spring of the Air and Its Effects* ([1660]). Consider the casual brilliance with which Boyle shows the successful functioning of the air pump and the air required for "small animals" to breathe. First, he reports that, having placed a "flesh-fly" in the container that is attached to the pump, "the fly, after some exsuctions of the air, dropped down from the side of the glass whereon she was walking." An earlier experiment had used a bee and, after the pump had operated for some time, the bee fell from the flowers that had been hung from the ceiling of the container. These experimental results, however, failed to distinguish between two plausible hypotheses that could account for the bee's and the fly's behavior, and Boyle knew it, claiming that a further experiment would be needed to determine "whether this fall of the bee, and the other insect, proceeded from the medium's being too thin for them to fly in, or barely from the weakness, and as it were swooning of the animals themselves" ([1660], p. 97). No matter which of the two explanatory hypotheses for falling one favors (that is, either no support from thin medium or swooning), the hypothesis not selected *was* a plausible rival hypothesis. So, additional experiments were run, the involuntary participants being a lark, a hen sparrow, and a mouse. In the latter three cases, the animals lapsed into unconsciousness within about ten minutes.

Boyle is assuming that a theoretical hypothesis can be tested by a further experiment, and that what separates a good hypothesis from a bad hypothesis is not just its truth value, but also its ability to unify. A theoretical hypothesis that can unify "the fall of the bee" and the other relevant observed phenomena — by appeal to the same unobservable cause(s) — is preferable to one that can't. It is a chief feature of experimentation that experiments be designed in such a way that they test a hypothesis against its most plausible rivals. The theoretical preference widely shown for explanations that unify otherwise disparate data is favorable to so-called explanationist accounts of justification. (Chapters 8 and 9 will return to this point, favoring an explanationist approach to justification and to epistemology itself.) In effect, we justifiably accept the unifying hypothesis relative to the pertinent data because it offers the best available explanation of the data in need of explanation.

Explanationism about justification is not especially technical or arcane. It figures not only in science, but also in law and leisure, among many other domains. If, for example, you hear sounds coming from the baseboard late at night (and not just any sounds — scratching sounds rather than, say, a Bach fugue), you might naturally believe that you have mice. If you not only hear scratching sounds, but also see small droppings, your conviction for the mouse hypothesis will doubtless increase. Why is this? A plausible reply: It would seem an improbable coincidence that the two events had independent causes — not inconceivable, of course, but improbable. So, the mouse hypothesis, however unsettling psychologically, unifies disparate observations. Even though the mouse is as yet unobserved by you, you conclude that you have a mouse problem. This is not an irresponsible conclusion. In fact, it might be decisively preferable to the skeptic's aversion to possible error.

The consistent skeptic might note the two pieces of evidence, but draw no conclusion, closing his eyes and hoping that, *if* there is a mouse, it will not be enjoying the granola in the closet. In the face of deprivation, the demanding skeptic still acts as we all do (or ought), and stores the granola in a mouse-proof container. Skeptics may thus face their most severe practical challenge when their food is at risk.

In legal settings, converging evidence carries much weight. When attempting to establish the presence of the defendant at the crime scene, jurors will find that eyewitness evidence and physical evidence (such as hair or blood), are together more persuasive than either taken individually. This is not a peculiar fact about the law, nor about jurors. The patterns of justification jurors find compelling are just the patterns that everyone else finds compelling. After all, we belong to the same population — and wise attorneys prepare accordingly. So the various possible sources of knowledge we have discussed, including perception, reason, and memory, can work together and with other sources to increase the justification for a belief. One last important source of knowledge is the testimony of other epistemic agents, or *knowers*, around us.

Testimony and Social Dependence

The search for justification, as suggested in Chapter 1, often takes us outside ourselves, to social and physical aspects of the world. Sometimes we must rely on others if we are to be epistemically responsible. The reliability of social dependence issues from the special position occupied by the person relied on. This special position can take a number of forms: technical expertise based on arcane theoretical information (for example, expertise in physics), practical expertise (for example, in plumbing or farming), and normal perceptual skills. A cell biologist's justification for her belief that her instruments are reliable, for instance, depends on a body of engineering knowledge outside the biologist's own expertise.

Epistemic social dependence is evident in other, more mundane contexts. According to a familiar approach to justification, a blind person can have justification for a belief that there is a ditch in his path even if the only source of evidence is the testimony of a sighted person. The source need not be human to be a reliable indicator of a ditch. A dog trained for use by blind people can provide the required justification. Some philosophers take such cases to illustrate that an ingredient central to justification is reliable indication. An expert can be reliable in his special area but no more reliable than a novice in another area. (We know philosophers who are clueless about changing the oil in their cars; politeness recommends silence on their other deficiencies.) Whether alleged experts merit deference depends, it seems, on their possession of evident *relevant* reliability, reliability in the relevant domain of belief formation. The recognition that epistemically relevant expertise or reliability is domain relative has prompted renewed attention to the social and cultural influences on justification.

A noteworthy means of justification and knowledge is called *triangulation* (see Trout 1998). It states that beliefs held on the basis of a greater number of independent methods are, in general, more reliable (or, likely to be true) than beliefs held on the basis of a single method. This notion of triangulation is found in science and common sense. It suggests that, if we come to the same conclusion by diverse methods, then the probability that this convergence is a coincidence may be correspondingly lower and perhaps even rationally negligible.

In contexts of testimony, triangulation occurs across a variety of disciplines and settings, soliciting expert reports from different individuals. Such a social balance can provide a check on bias. Social rationality of this sort is especially instructive here, for rationality is most often characterized as a property of an individual. If one successfully follows inductive or deductive rules, one is said to be rational. This conception models rationality on individual problem-solving. The rationality of groups, however, does not emerge in any simple way from the rational decision processes of individuals.

The rationality of a scientific community offers a case in point. One goal (among others) of a scientific community may be to create a vaccine. To achieve this goal, the scientific community must farm out separate tasks to various experts. The selected experts may themselves have diverse goals. One goal may be sheer fame, another the accumulation of research to secure a grant (and with it, more research grants). In fact, many of the experts may be utterly insensitive to the overarching goals of the research program. The goal of much research on pasteurization, for example, was to promote the production of good wine, while perhaps individual scientists had as their goals the understanding of chemical and cellular processes of fermentation.

There are various ways that the intellectual professions, as groups, attempt to secure their respective group goals. One such way used in the sciences and the humanities is peer review, whereby a number of specialists judge the competence and value of a work considered for public distribution. Reviewers often have somewhat different training, and this can supply the kind of diverse testing wrought by triangulation. Peer review, when suitably regulated, can be conceived of as a social process of bias correction and error detection. If the diverse perspectives represented by peer review are regarded as an epistemic value, then the focus of feminist epistemology on diverse perspectives can be understood as a similar directive for social triangulation. Feminist epistemology is itself a diverse intellectual movement, but one of its recurring themes grounds justification in salient social and psychological aspects of human culture.

Feminist epistemology, like most intellectual movements, includes both negative (or, critical) and positive projects. It attempts both to locate difficulties with current views and to articulate improvements and alternatives. As part of the critical project, some feminist philosophers identify and describe the nature of arguably patriarchal institutions (such as science and the university) that have shaped our efforts to acquire public and objective knowledge. They have identified the tendency in the history of science to objectify nature, to present knowers as standing outside of nature and of any community. In addition, they have suggested that this tendency is patriarchal or categorically "male" in that it favors controlling rather than cooperating with the world; it favors bending nature to the investigator's independent will.

Some feminist epistemologists have concentrated on the subjective aspects of knowledge that may be sexually specific or gendered. The ability to know what giving birth is like, for example, results from the biological character of a woman's body. Epistemology has long been concerned with the nature of subjective experiences. Philosophers thus have investigated whether a person can have the concept of a certain experience "by description" while lacking the experience itself. Can a blind person, for instance, know what red is like, simply by knowing what normally happens physiologically in a human who sees red? The epistemic distinctiveness of biology-based experiences merits careful attention from epistemologists.

Some feminists have focused on the socially and culturally situated character of a person's understanding of self and world. For example, the epistemic situation of an eleventh-century female peasant, or that of an eighteenth-century slave in the United States, cannot fully be appreciated through sheer philosophical rumination by a contemporary white male, even after much historical study and contemplative effort. It does not follow that we must abandon all hope of understanding others. The point is rather that we should not blithely assume that the actual relations one bears to the world (and thus to other knowers) are irrelevant to the formulation of epistemic concepts and principles. The social relations regulating some epistemic processes are subtle and complex. Feminist epistemologists have tried to characterize such relations in their work on epistemic communities.

The social settings in which knowledge arises take us beyond feminist epistemology, to a general movement in the social studies of knowledge. Research on the practices of science, associated with a discipline sometimes called "science studies," advances elaborate descriptions of the epistemological features of scientific settings. Social and psychological taxonomies and distinctions, all human constructions, abound in such research. We should keep in mind, however, that epistemology is also about the way these practices are connected to the world. There is no real doubt that much knowledge is mediated by involvement in institutions — human, dateable, culturally specific institutions.

The interesting question is whether, and if so how, institutions aid in the acquisition of beliefs that are approximately true. Institutions are, of course, social organizations, consolidating all the ideological biases that cognizing flesh is heir to. Therefore, the history of scientific knowledge leaves us with difficult questions. If we agree that many of the scientific institutions of Europe systematically discriminated against women — the various academies were typically exclusive clubs for educated white gentlemen — then we are faced with the fact that the enormously successful, truth-conducive institution of Western science has been sexist and racist. This recognition may challenge the Enlightenment sentiment that the truth is always emancipatory. We might resolve the threatening tension by conceiving of scientific institutions as functionally complex, and by adding that the causal structures in nature explored by science are similarly complex. This means, among other things, that a scientific institution may serve some aims better than others over different periods of time.

The fact of the social dependence of much knowledge has striking consequences. Philosophers have traditionally announced the virtues of intellectual self-reliance. If, however, knowledge typically has ineliminably social and cultural aspects, the nature of intellectual self-reliance must be reconceived. We can be intellectually autonomous in the sense that we must identify those with the relevant expertise, but we cannot be intellectually autonomous in the sense that we can justifiably decide substantial technical issues outside our areas of expertise. As a result, an adequate epistemology must be socially sensitive, ever attentive to expert evidence arising from various sectors of society.

Debates about the relative importance of social sources of knowledge versus the prospects for epistemic self-reliance resemble in some ways the debates over empiricism and rationalism. Epistemologists want to know where knowledge comes from and how we acquire it. We all want to know, for example, whether all knowledge derives ultimately from sense experience, because the answer to this question will profoundly influence what methods of justification for knowledge claims are relevant. We also want to know how knowledge gets transmitted socially and how large bodies of knowledge can thereby emerge and apparently acquire a life of their own independent of any particular knower. There is a loose sense, for example, in which there is a huge stockpile of "knowledge" in the Library of Congress greater than any particular human knower could ever grasp.

In sum, then, we have seen in our study of sources of knowledge that forces pull us in opposite directions, both toward epistemic self-reliance and away from it. On the one hand, we emphasize epistemic self-reliance because we realize that ultimately "the buck stops here." That is, each one of us is an epistemic agent who must determine what to believe just from one's available *personal* sources of knowledge, such as perception, reason and memory. On the other hand, we realize the greatly increased power of a collective social pursuit of knowledge, reaching far beyond what any individual human could accomplish. We also realize how much we depend on others for even much mundane knowledge we have of the world.

The unifying concern in our studies of the sources of knowledge is the twofold goal of knowing significant truths and avoiding error. The social dependence of knowledge helps us greatly in acquiring significant truths, and methods such as triangulation protect us (at least, according to many epistemologists) from having too many false beliefs. The pursuit of significant truths and the attempt to avoid false beliefs require the formation of beliefs in a *rational* way. That is, rationality is a necessary ingredient in our twofold epistemic goal, and we turn now to this important topic.

7

Rationality

PRELIMINARY DISTINCTIONS

Having identified some main cognitive sources, we must ask whether, and if so in what sense, the beliefs delivered by those sources are rational. People seeking true beliefs usually desire to be rational in achieving their cognitive goal. For instance, they are not satisfied with acquiring truth coincidentally or haphazardly. Philosophers, too, have typically aspired to be rational in their beliefs and decisions, but have not thereby sought exactly the same thing.

Portrayed broadly, rationality is reasonableness, but not all philosophers take rationality as dependent on reasons. Likewise, not all philosophers have a common understanding of reasons or of reasonableness. Some theorists consider rationality to obtain in cases that lack countervailing reasons against what has rationality. That is, rationality, according to some theorists, can be characterized only in terms of what is *not irrational*. (They thus countenance rationality as, in effect, a default status.) In ordinary parlance, persons themselves can have rationality; so, too, can beliefs, desires, intentions, and actions, among other things. The rationality appropriate to action is practical (determining what it is rational *to do*), whereas the rationality characteristic of beliefs is, in the language of some philosophers, theoretical (determining what it is rational *to believe*).

Many philosophers understand epistemic justification as determined just by the evidence one has. On that view, rationality will be irreducible to justification, because rationality extends to considerations about how one should acquire new evidence as well as re-evaluate current evidence (say, as biased or otherwise misleading). In addition, contemporary research on rationality attends to how people actually form beliefs and make decisions. Such empirical research illuminates the nature of human rationality and clarifies questions about the correct standards for evaluating human rationality.

Many philosophers deem rationality as *instrumental*, or goal-oriented, as opposed to goal-determining. You have rationality, according to some of these philosophers, in virtue of doing your best, or at least doing what you appropriately think adequate, to achieve your goals. For example, if your goal is to quench your thirst, it is rational for you to get a glass of water. If ultimate goals are not themselves subject to assessments of rationality, then rationality is *purely* instrumental, in a manner associated with David Hume's philosophy. Rationality, according to Hume, does not require any particular substantive goals of its own, but consists rather in the proper pursuit of one's ultimate goals, *whatever* those goals happen to be. Many decision-theoretic and economic approaches to rationality are purely instrumentalist.

If ultimate goals, such as quenching thirst, becoming rich, or overthrowing the government, are susceptible to rational assessment, as an Aristotelian tradition and a Kantian tradition maintain, then rationality is not purely instrumental. The latter two traditions regard certain rather specific (kinds of) goals, such as human well-being, as essential to rationality, or intrinsically rational. Philosophers in this tradition would distinguish rational goals, such as quenching thirst or having valuable friendships, from irrational goals, such as destroying innocent lives. Their *sub-stantialist* approach to rationality lost considerable influence, however, with the rise of modern decision theory.

When relevant goals concern the acquisition of (informative) truth and the avoidance of falsehood, as they do in much scientific research and in other forms of investigation, so-called *epistemic* rationality is at issue. Otherwise, some species of *nonepistemic* rationality is under consideration. We can individuate species of nonepistemic rationality by the kind of goal in view: moral (pursuing a moral good), prudential (pursuing a practical good, such as pleasure or happiness), political (pursuing a political objective), economic (pursuing wealth), aesthetic (pursuing beauty), or some other kind of goal.

Although the standards of rationality are not uniformly epistemic, epistemic rationality can play a role even in what some call nonepistemic rationality. Regarding economic rationality, for instance, a person seeking such rationality will, at least under ordinary conditions, aspire to epistemically rational beliefs concerning what will achieve the relevant economic goals. In other words, we want our beliefs about how to achieve our economic goals (such as avoiding poverty with fair distribution of wealth) to be rational with respect to our epistemic goal of acquiring truth and avoiding falsehood. Similar points apply to other species of nonepistemic rationality. A comprehensive account of rationality will characterize epistemic and nonepistemic rationality, as well as corresponding kinds of irrationality (for example, weakness of will).

It is customary to distinguish what is rationally required, or obligatory, from what is rationally permissible. If an action or belief is rationally required, or obligatory, then it is irrational not to perform the action or hold the belief. For example, if it is rationally required for a person to pursue his or her own well-being, then performing an action that brings harm to oneself is irrational (assuming there are no other, countervailing reasons making the action at least rationally permissible). Likewise, if you believe that only human beings use complex language and that Fido is not a human, you are rationally required to believe that Fido does not use complex language, at least if you *consider* that proposition and understand that it follows deductively from your prior beliefs. Failing to believe it would be irrational under such conditions.

Some actions and beliefs are rationally permissible without being rationally required. It is not irrational, for example, to see a new movie if you wish (under normal circumstances), and it is not irrational to refrain from seeing it. Either action is rational in the sense of being rationally permissible. According to many theorists, we are not *required* to believe all the deductive consequences of our beliefs, because some of them are too difficult to comprehend without a great deal of effort. Such beliefs would be rationally *permitted*, however, if one were to work hard enough to comprehend them.

Few theorists today suppose that rationality is distinctively human. Our perceptual and cognitive systems are capable of processing enormous amounts of information, but this is true for all higher organisms, such as dogs, dolphins, chimpanzees, and humans. Higher organisms are able to process information in a way that tends to preserve truth-conducive features of beliefs and to identify ways of satisfying desires. In short, higher organisms apparently are capable of instrumental rationality, even though their cognitive abilities vary across some species. By contrast, Aristotle had suggested that we humans are uniquely adept at rationally organizing information and drawing inferences. Descartes likewise suggested that we are uniquely rational among living things.

Whatever favor evolution has shown higher cognitive organisms, it is clear that we are intelligent: We can devise and execute highly effective strategies to achieve our goals, however mundane or technical. Our sensory systems enable us to avoid injury and to spot sustenance by making subtle discriminations among conditions differing in degrees of desirability. Our cognitive capacities regulate intelligent, rational conduct.

We can illuminate relations between epistemology and the theory of rationality by examining some phenomena central to much intellectual inquiry: deduction, induction, normative and descriptive assessment, bias, and sensitivity to cultural and social context.

We shall confront conflicting conceptions of rationality, with one conception implying that a belief of a particular culture is irrational and another conception implying that it is rational. Once the flavor of such a dispute is conveyed, some will be tempted to conclude that we cannot resolve disputes about what is rational. One supposed ground for such a conclusion is that a belief regarded as rational by one person or by one culture simply *is* rational. This is a relativistic outlook with troublesome consequences. It makes rationality too easy to acquire and no different in kind from mere opinion. If rationality is no more than a matter of mere opinion, we should jettison the honorific label "rational" and make do with talk of mere opinion. At least honesty would then be served.

When ultimate goals are not at issue, two people who disagree about what to believe can often be shown whether and how their beliefs should be revised in light of the evidence. Research on human judgment under risk and uncertainty suggests how some such disputes can be resolved. The base-rate fallacy, availability bias, and in general the violation of Bayes's Theorem all represent the violation of certain normative rules pertinent to rationality. The penultimate section of this chapter will return to this matter.

RATIONAL INFERENCE: NORMATIVE AND DESCRIPTIVE

If theories of rationality are about anything, they are about making epistemically responsible inferences in light of available evidence. This talk of responsibility makes rationality a topic of evaluation. So, it is no surprise to find theories of rational decision and judgment rife with normative notions, attributions of *good* reasoning, *sound* judgment, etc. Even so, the factors that contribute to rational decision in any particular case can have such diverse sources that it is difficult to offer a general definition of rationality. An inference can be inductive or deductive, it could depend on expertise or not, it may or may not demand the integration of affective (that is, emotional) with cognitive states. Further, many different types of phenomena, such as beliefs, desires, intentions, decisions, and goals, among other things, can be evaluated as rational or irrational.

The evaluation of behavior as rational or irrational is sometimes easy to determine when it is based on canons of deduction, such as *modus ponens,* or abstract inductive rules, such as the central limit theorem. Most patterns of reasoning, however, are not so formally evaluable. In common cases, we hold ourselves and others responsible for flouting widely known, substantial facts of almost every conceivable kind. Charges of irrationality against the following views should thus have a familiar ring, each view being dubbed "irrational" for special reasons:

> "I didn't know whether the spider on me was poisonous, so I hit it." This strategy would be regarded as irrational because it is irresponsible about how to achieve one's goal—in this case, the goal of not being bitten—and it makes poor use of widely available information.

> "I bought the ring on a credit card, so it's not as though I will have to pay for it." Often one's desires for an end can be so overpowering that one does not have the emotional strength to acknowledge the barriers to achieving that end. This source of irrationality may be said to be affect-generated.

> "I am the lizard king." Some beliefs are irrational because they are delusional; the person cannot distinguish between fantasy and reality.

> "I took it as a good omen that the person I just met had the same birthday as I do." Many events seem remarkable, salient, or generally significant, because their occurrence would otherwise be thought improbable. This fact makes people prone to various sorts of inductive errors such as the base-rate fallacy and the availability bias (to be discussed in this chapter).

These examples illustrate the normativity of standard charges of irrationality.

Traditional conceptions of rationality cast rational inference as neutral regarding subject matter. From philosophical tradition, two ideals of rationality have emerged: deductive and inductive. In both cases, the guiding idea is that there are rules whose proper application generates a conclusion that is rationally acceptable.

The normal product of reasoning is an argument, a finite series of statements (premises) offered in support of another statement (conclusion). Many arguments are *inductive*; the premises offer probabilistic support for the conclusion, and on those grounds, the conclusion has a certain *probability* of being true. For example:

1. The sun has risen every day in the past. So,
2. The sun will probably rise tomorrow.

   or

1. This jar of mixed marbles has a 95:5 ratio of red to green marbles. So,
2. A person will probably select a red marble on a blind trial.

In inductive arguments, the conclusion goes considerably beyond the information contained in the premises; still, inductive inference can be rational.

Deductive arguments involve reasoning that is *conclusive* in a certain respect. When reasoning deductively, you want your argument to be, at the very least, deductively *valid*. Deductively valid arguments are such that *if* the premises of the argument are true, then the conclusion must be true too. Put another way, it is logically impossible for the premises of a deductively valid argument to be true and the conclusion to be false. In this sense, the information contained in the conclusion of a valid deductive argument does not go beyond the information contained in the premises. For example:

1. Talc is the hardest mineral on Moh's hardness scale.
2. The hardest mineral on Moh's hardness scale is used in cheap jewelry. So,
3. Talc is used in cheap jewelry.

This argument is deductively valid, since the conclusion would be true if the premises were true. Even so, the premises and the conclusion are false. Therefore, valid arguments can have false premises and false conclusions. An argument has the property of deductive validity if its structure is such that the relation between premises and conclusion is truth-preserving, but the premises themselves need not be true.

An argument is *sound* if it is valid and has true premises. For example:

1. Diamond is the hardest mineral on Moh's hardness scale.
2. The hardest mineral on Moh's hardness scale is used in expensive jewelry. So,
3. Diamond is used in expensive jewelry.

Two points are noteworthy. First, all inductive arguments (many of which are rational arguments) are deductively invalid. Second, although our initial concern should be with constructing valid arguments, we should aim for the argument to have true premises and thus to be sound as well.

In keeping with a formal model of deliberative rationality, some theorists have advanced a formal principle of instrumental rationality, as follows:

> *Principle of Instrumental Rationality:* If you intend that a situation, X, occur and you believe, in agreement with your evidence, that another situation, Y, is the most effective means to X, then you rationally should aim to have Y occur.

This principle of rational deliberation does not require that we know what exact situations "X" and "Y" stand for. At least initially, the principle of instrumental rationality promises a neutral attitude toward goals, and so avoids familiar problems that arise when rationality requires people to agree about ends, or goals. Given the principle of instrumental rationality, people can disagree about the value or desirability of X (X could be one's getting a Harley, a house, or a Husky), but agree that bringing about Y is the best way to achieve X.

Cases of instrumentally rational conduct seem familiar enough: If we intend to have a cold drink, and we believe, in agreement with our evidence, that the best way to get a cold drink is to go to the refrigerator, then we reasonably decide to make the trip to the refrigerator. Still, it is important to ask what the best method—the most rational method—is for the handling of complex information.

Our principle of instrumental rationality seems attractive at face value, if only because it does not require a judgment about the desirability of ends and so apparently does not import substantive value commitments (concerning, for example, the immorality of a certain end) into an already complicated terrain. We can ask how efficiently an agent executed an intended plan relative to an end, no matter how peculiar or offensive we may find the agent's ends. Psychologists inevitably raise questions about normal and pathological behavior and thus about the conditions suitable for human flourishing. In this connection, psychologists often assess the claim that a certain action is rational in light of the action's contribution to goal satisfaction. As the history of psychology illustrates, this is not an unambiguous task, for there is often tension between short-term and long-term satisfaction of goals. For instance, it may give you giddy satisfaction for moments during dessert to eat an entire three-pound fruitcake, but this overeating will also make you dismally sick for several hours thereafter. (A friendly warning: Please refrain from testing this at home.) Moreover, what counts as an effective means to an end, let alone the most effective means, is itself often disputable. So, even when we fill in variables "X" and "Y," disagreements may persist concerning the best way to achieve X. In any case, even a principle of instrumental rationality involves a normative notion of effectiveness concerning means to ends. No technical maneuver of distinction drawing can remove the normative notion of effectiveness pertinent to instrumental rationality.

Regarding the rational assessment of ends, a cigarette can give some people unsurpassed satisfaction, even if it is not in their long-term interest to smoke. If some people are willing to die earlier than they otherwise would have in exchange for years of smoking enjoyment, they could not be faulted for being instrumentally irrational—as long as the pertinent calculations have been made. Only a value theory that makes substantial claims about the character of human flourishing and happiness can supply the basis for a plausible argument that it is not in your objective long-term interest to smoke.

Remaining doubt about the rationality of a decision to smoke may stem from a suspicion, not without foundation, that such a decision cannot really be made *effectively*. According to this suspicion, individuals cannot calculate the disutility (or whatever value one wants to use) of years of pain or of early death. There are various reasons for this difficulty, such as a difficulty in selecting appropriate units of measurement (happiness, pleasure, usefulness, etc.) and a difficulty in having the proper experiential and cognitive basis for making the calculation. Regarding the latter issue, it is worth asking what experiences could possibly equip persons with the information required to determine intelligently that their pleasure from smoking is greater than the pain of unknown severity and duration.

Given agreement on a goal, we can raise the interesting question whether people are reliable in processing information required to secure that goal. This is not just an interesting question; it is partly empirical as well. Although common wisdom and philosophical tradition have assumed that people are at least instrumentally rational, empirical research has raised questions about how rational people actually are.

CONSISTENCY AND WAYWARD BELIEFS

A conception of rationality is operative whenever we attempt to explain behavior in the familiar way — by attributing beliefs and desires. On this view, our mental states have contents, and those contents represent the world in a certain way. To explain someone else's behavior, thereby identifying a rationale for it, we must characterize the contents of that person's mental states.

People of certain cultures develop strategies of inference unfamiliar to those from other cultures. When judging the rationality of such culturally unfamiliar principles, we face a difficulty. What if our own theoretical commitments cause us to regard a crucial premise in their belief system as being false? Do we then regard them as holding irrational views? Some cultural traditions, for instance, include a belief that some individuals are unique in possessing what we would regard as supernatural powers, such as the powers of witchcraft. Many theorists hold that a belief in the powers of witchcraft requires an unduly immaterialist conception of the world — given its implication that nonphysical things influence the causal order of the natural world.

Philosophers widely agree that we should hold beliefs that are at least consistent, particularly that we should not embrace contradictory views. When interpreting alien cultures, however, it is not a simple matter for us to determine when a set of beliefs is internally inconsistent. We find this point in various anthropologists and in Quine, who casts a consistency constraint in terms of translation:

> To take the extreme case, let us suppose that certain natives are said to accept as true certain sentences translatable in the form "P and not-P." Now this claim is absurd under our semantic criteria. And, not to be dogmatic about them, what criteria might one prefer? Wanton translation can make natives sound as queer as one pleases. Better translation imposes our logic upon them. . . . (Quine 1960, p. 58)

The attribution of beliefs and preferences to others — often from a radically different culture or epoch — challenges us to translate their language into language we can understand. Let's turn to a concrete case.

The anthropologist Edward Evans-Pritchard reported that witchcraft beliefs played a pervasive role in regulating conduct among the Azande (see Evans-Pritchard 1972, chaps. 1–4). It may seem that Zande beliefs ("Zande" is the adjectival form) about witchcraft are irrational once we consider the apparent contradiction identified by Evans-Pritchard. The Azande believe in a "witchcraft substance" that would be observable in a witch's intestines during postmortem examination. They also believe that the status of being a witch is handed down by inheritance from witches to their offspring. These beliefs should enable the

Azande to conclude, after some postmortem testing of intestines, that the offspring of a certain witch are witches too. The Azande, however, sometimes remain undecided about the status of off-spring of witches, even after the relevant testing. One might thus conclude that the Azande are irrational.

Two lines of reply are noteworthy. First, Peter Winch (1964) has denied that the Azande are irrational on the ground that Zande ideas of witchcraft do not offer a theoretical system by which the Azande try to acquire a quasi-scientific understanding of the world. As a result, Winch recommends that we not try to press Zande thinking to a contradiction. Charles Taylor (1982) finds Winch's reply inadequate, on the ground that the Azande would be opposed to a contradiction in their belief system, even if they were not interested in formulating a theoretical under-standing of the world. Taylor notes that the Azande could have replied to the charge of contradiction as follows: "Witch power is mysterious; it doesn't operate according to the exceptionless laws that you Europeans take as the basis of what you call science. But only if you assume this does the contradiction arise" (1982, p. 89). Taylor thus proposes that the apparent contradictions could be removed if we recast the Zande claims about witches and witchcraft in rigorous theoretical language, noting the rele-vant exceptions.

Another matter concerns whether an explanation can *rationalize* the belief in witches. What role, if any, does belief in the heritabil-ity of witchcraft play in Zande society? The traditional explana-tion makes it possible for the belief in witches to be rational even if individual believers are unaware of the beneficial effects their beliefs have. According to Evans-Pritchard, father-son heritability of being a witch serves to maintain kinship relations by directing witchcraft accusations away from the family, where claims to com-pensation cannot be collected. In accusing the father of witch-craft, the son could be impugning himself as well. Moreover, since witchcraft accusations are directed to nonkin and carry with them a claim to retributive courtesy and consideration, they have the effect of maintaining social bonds by balancing claims against one another. In short, the belief that witchcraft follows the male line serves the objective function of contributing to the stability of social relations among the Azande.

Questionable stabilizing beliefs are not uncommon in European and American cultures. The belief that redemption is secured through hard work, for example, is widely explained functionally, in terms of the contribution it makes to the production of a pliant labor pool. Individuals holding this belief do not necessarily work hard because they believe that by doing so they will weaken the bargaining power of labor or create a stronger economy — even if this is the effect. Beliefs can have a valuable, and rationally explainable, social function even when the relevant believers are themselves unclear on that function. Whether the relevant believers, in that case, would themselves be rational in holding the beliefs in question will depend on how demanding our notion of rationality is regarding first-person access to what rationalizes a belief or an action. An appeal to firm intuitions, in any case, will not settle this matter for all participants to the dispute. Let's pursue the matter of irrationality further, in connection with some apparently widespread errors of human judgment.

RATIONALITY AND DECISION UNDER UNCERTAINTY

No matter what we think of the Zande belief system, we might wonder whether the social stability thereby gained could be achieved by more effective, or more optimal, means. Whenever people perform suboptimally, there are at least two ready explanations: (a) defective thought processes are present; and (b) specific task demands interfere with the disposition toward otherwise rational judgment. So, what are we to conclude about suboptimal performance? On what basis can we effectively criticize errant behavior and preserve the normative dimension of rationality?

Modern decision theory assumes that, in satisfying certain consistency and completeness requirements, a person's preferences toward the possible outcomes of available actions will determine, at least in part, what actions are rational for that person by determining the personal utility of outcomes of those actions. In rational decision-making under *certainty*, one definitely knows the outcomes of available actions. In decision-making under *risk*, one can assign only various definite probabilities less than one to the outcomes of available actions. So-called Bayesians about decision-making assume that the relevant probabilities are subjective in that they are determined by a decision-maker's *beliefs*. In decision-making under *uncertainty*, one lacks information about states of the world relevant to one's decision, and thus cannot assign even definite probabilities to the outcomes of available actions.

Acknowledging that rationality is purely instrumental (and thus that even Hitler's Nazi objectives are not necessarily rationally flawed), Herbert Simon (1983) has faulted modern decision theory on the ground that humans rarely have available the facts, consistent preferences, and reasoning power required by standard decision theory. He contends that human rationality is "bounded" in that it does not require utility maximization or even consistency. It rather requires the application of a certain range of personal values (or, preferences) to resolve fairly specific problems one faces, in a way that is *satisfactory*, rather than optimal, for one. Simon thus relies on actual human limitations to constrain his account of rationality.

Contemporary theorists divide over the significance of human psychological limitations for an account of rationality. The controversy turns on just how idealized principles for rationality should be. This raises the important issue of what exactly makes some principles of rationality true and others false. If principles of rationality are not just stipulative definitions (*establishing* what rationality is), this issue merits more attention from philosophers than it has received. Neglect of this meta-philosophical issue leaves the theory of rationality as a subject of ongoing philosophical controversy.

Theorists of rationality have offered a number of rules for forming beliefs based on probabilistic reasoning. One of the most famous rules is Bayes's theorem. A key implication of Bayes's theorem is that the probability of a belief *given certain evidence* is proportional to the product of the probability of the evidence *assuming the truth of the belief* and the probability of the belief independently of the particular evidence at hand, or the so-called *prior probability* of the belief. For example, if there are two jars containing black and white marbles and someone has drawn a black marble from one of the jars, you can assess the probability that it came from the first jar if you know the initial contents of both jars. If the first jar was, say, 95 percent black and the second jar was 95 percent white, then it is much more likely that the observed black marble was drawn from the first jar than from the second. (More specifically, the probability of the belief given the evidence equals the aforementioned product divided by the probability of the evidence independently of the belief in question, or the prior probability of the evidence.)

Bayes's theorem and the conception of rationality it favors are important for two reasons. First, they have been enormously influential in a variety of fields, such as confirmation theory in the philosophy of science, rational decision theory, and the formal theory of learning. Second, they represent a certain *normative* approach to rational decision-making. They offer, according to many theorists, a rule by which one rationally *ought* to update one's level of epistemic commitment (or degree of belief) concerning a particular hypothesis in light of new evidence. Other normative theories of decision-making abound (such as Herbert Simon's, mentioned previously), but Bayesianism has been especially resilient.

Because probability values can be assigned to a background theory, many theorists suppose that Bayes's theorem can accommodate the role of background knowledge in rational decision-making. In psychology, Bayesian models have been advanced to elucidate the decision-making of small groups of experts and of laypeople, such as juries and management teams. A prevalent assumption is that Bayes's theorem is itself theoretically neutral in that it applies no matter what the subject matter. The idea that Bayesian inference (just one rule among many) should produce plausible conclusions in one domain (for example, economics) but not in another (for example, political science) gets no serious attention in some circles.

As a *description* of our actual inferential procedures, Bayesianism fails in principle and in detail. Neither laypeople nor scientists nor specialists of other kinds consistently update their epistemic commitments according to Bayesian strictures. Because humans routinely violate Bayesian rules, Bayesians have retreated from descriptive pretensions and rested content with the *normative* claim that we *ought* to reason as Bayesians — that our inferences would be more rational if we did so. The latter claim is testable, and a number of people have picked up the gauntlet. Many psychologists and statisticians have examined this matter experimentally. We shall sketch some of their results highlighting cognitive tendencies that are apparently irrational.

Base-Rate Fallacy

If an inference is to be rational, it must be sensitive to the relationship between properties or classes mentioned in its premises. Some of these classes reflect relations of causal dependence, and statistical evidence is often used in an attempt to establish the extent and direction of such causal dependence. If we wish, for example, to establish that the stress of being a commercial pilot causes heart disease, we need to examine the frequency of heart disease among commercial pilots. We might find that 14 percent of commercial pilots suffer heart disease, and conclude that commercial piloting and heart disease are causally related. Theorists sometimes use narrative methods to report, by appeal to a percentage or rate, the frequency of a certain event without specifying the percentage range that should merit a causal claim.

For the support of a causal claim about a particular property in a population, however, we need to *compare* the relative frequency of this property in the population (14 percent in this case) to the frequency of that property *in the general population*. The latter measure is called the *base rate*. If we infer that the occupational stress of piloting causes heart disease but the heart disease rate for the general population is 12 percent, our conclusion would be the result of what is called the base-rate fallacy. The rate among pilots does not diverge *significantly* from the rate among the population generally. Specialists and nonspecialists often commit this fallacy by inferring a causal connection based merely on an observed correlation without comparing the correlation to the appropriate base rate. (For details see Tversky and Kahneman 1974.)

Availability Bias

Another apparently irrational cognitive tendency also concerns causal inference. When reasoning casually, we typically draw from a body of experiences that has not been organized with accurate statistical representation in mind. Memory allows only certain experiences to be retained, most often because they are especially memorable or *available.* According to one current theory, an *availability heuristic* is employed whenever someone "estimates frequency or probability by the ease with which instances or associations could be brought to mind" (Tversky and Kahneman 1973, p. 208). Given a wide range of experimental studies (for a survey, see Tversky and Kahneman 1973; Gilovich 1991), we cannot seriously doubt that the outcomes of people's reasoning are often shaped by something like an availability bias. A range of psychological phenomena, in addition to recency and order effects, make us prone to an availability bias.

In fact, the availability bias often interacts with the base-rate fallacy. It is common, for example, to find the following sort of schematic explanation for traditions of superstition:

> The cultures in question were marked by scarcity and disease. It is no wonder that rituals and institutions of supernatural control should have evolved within such cultures as insulation from a harsh and capricious environment as well as from the threat of disease.

Of course, it is important to know the base rate in each population considered. In a world where people routinely (certainly with higher relative frequency than at present) died of starvation and of diseases we can now cure, the population may have been habituated to the starvation and disease base rates of their epoch.

One of the most powerful influences prompting an availability bias is the phenomenon of *framing*. Framing is the process whereby a problem is presented to an audience, preparing them to see a certain range of possible options, solutions, evidential bearing, and so on. The audience's intellectual habits and explanatory expectations allow carefully framed narrative descriptions to yield defective inductions. Framing typically gets the reader or listener to ignore important quantitative, sampling information. A number of studies have shown that whether subjects find an option acceptable or not depends on how the alternatives are presented rather than on quantitative information that, on the typical paradigm of these studies, ensures equally probable alternatives.

The following passage is representative of a wide range of instances of framing:

> Respondents in a telephone interview evaluated the fairness of an action described in the following vignette, which was presented in two versions that differed only in the bracketed clauses.
>
> > A company is making a small profit. It is located in a community experiencing a recession with substantial unemployment [but no inflation/and inflation of 12 percent]. The company decides to [decrease wages and salaries 7 percent/increase salaries only 5 percent] this year.
>
> Although the loss of real income is very similar in the two versions, the proportion of respondents who judged the action of the company "unfair" or "very unfair" was 62 percent for a nominal reduction but only 22 percent for a nominal increase. (Tversky and Kahneman 1986, pp. 71–72)

Explanation and theory play just such a framing role, making some options available, and foreclosing others. Unless explanation is regulated by the relevant properties of the studied population, framing will lead to biases in the assessment of evidence.

Confirmation Bias

Laypeople are prone to at least two types of biases directly related to confirmation, and there is little reason to suppose that scientists differ in this respect. In the most famous study (Lord, Ross, and Lepper 1979), two groups of subjects were assembled. One group expressed strong belief in the deterrent effect of capital punishment, and the other expressed strong belief that capital punishment had no deterrent value. Subjects were divided so that they first read the method and results of an experimental study supporting their respective positions, and then they read the method and results of an experiment that opposed their views. For all subjects, one study compared murder rates for states before and after the introduction of capital punishment (called a "panel" design) and the other compared murder rates contemporaneously (a "concurrent" design) in states with and states without capital punishment. The experiment was arranged so that, for half of the subjects the concurrent design study supported their view and the panel design opposed it, and for the other half it was exactly the opposite (see Nisbett and Ross 1980).

Three results are noteworthy. First, subjects found "more convincing" whichever study supported their original view, whether the design was panel or concurrent. They reported recognizing the methodological defects only of the design that opposed their favored conclusion. Second, subjects' beliefs were strengthened when the study supported their view, whether the design was panel or concurrent; at the same time, the initial belief was largely unaffected by studies opposing the subject's original position. Third, not only did the clear expression of an opposing view fail to undermine subjects' confidence in their original views, subjects were *more* committed to their original view after having read both analyses.

Confirmation bias interacts with the availability heuristic in research done by Fischoff (1991). Researchers who expected to see a certain phenomenon tended to overestimate the frequency of confirming instances of their hypotheses. The explanation given for this fact turns on the availability heuristic, because matches between theory and data are thought to be more psychologically salient than mismatches.

Judgment Under Uncertainty and Task Demands

Deductive models of rationality characterize reasoning in terms of the formal derivation of a conclusion from the contents of the premises. Here the standard of deductive validity is all the normativity required. The most famous research on fallacies of deductive reasoning was initiated by Wason and Johnson-Laird (1972). According to one version of their standard "selection task," subjects are asked to determine whether a particular deductive rule, *If P then Q,* is violated in the presentation of specially prepared cards. The rule here is violated only when *P* is true and *Q* is false. Such logical rules, whether inductive or deductive, apply no matter what the subject matter or context. The generality of general purpose rules does not come for free. There are many competencies that cannot be adequately constrained by such rules. For example, Cosmides and Tooby (1992) claim that the "*If P then Q*" rule is too weak to explain how we can spot cheaters in social contract settings.

One abstract version of the selection task concerns the alphanumeric rule. In the standard task, subjects are presented with four cards:

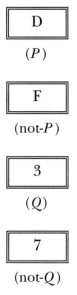

Subjects were told that part of their new clerical job is to make certain that particular documents have been handled correctly. There is an "alphanumeric rule" that must be followed. They are told: "If the person has a 'D' rating, then his documents must be marked code '3'." One side of the card has a letter, the other has a number. Which card(s) do you need to turn over to see if the rule has been violated? In effect, subjects are being asked to detect violations of conditional rules. The abstract logical form of the offending violation is "P & not-Q." In more than twenty years of testing people on the logical version of this problem, however, less than 25 percent of subjects get the correct answer to this abstract question. Moreover, none of the versions of the logical task, familiar or unfamiliar, received impressive performance.

Performance did improve on more concrete tasks, particularly with reasoning about social contracts of various sorts. Consider the following experimental setting, called *The Drinking Age Problem*. Subjects are told that, as part of a crackdown against drunk driving, law enforcement officials in Massachusetts are revoking liquor licenses without hesitation. Every subject is told that, as a bouncer in a Boston bar, you'll be fired unless you enforce the following law:

If a person is drinking beer, then he or she must be over 20 years old.
  (*If*   *P*   *then*   *Q)*

Subjects are then told that the cards below have information about four people sitting at a table in your bar. Each card represents one of those people. One side of a card tells what a person is drinking and the other side of the card tells that person's age. Finally, subjects are told to indicate only those card(s) that need to be turned over in order to see whether any of these people are breaking the law.

drinking beer
(*P*)

drinking coke
(not-*P*)

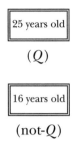

(Q)

$(\text{not-}Q)$

Therefore, while the original selection task is noticeably abstract, later research raised the question of whether the content of the relevant subject matter might affect performance (such as content to which the abstract selection task is noticeably insensitive). In fact, some content did affect performance. When addressing the formal issue of whether "*If P then Q*" was violated, subjects did not do well finding violations of such abstract rules, but they were good at identifying violations of conditional rules that express concrete social contracts (see Griggs and Cox 1982).

In one task, subjects are told that it is their job to enforce the following law:

Rule 1:   Standard Social Contract: "If you take the benefit, then you pay the cost." (If P then Q.)

Rule 2:   Switched Social Contract: "If you pay the cost, then you take the benefit." (If P then Q.)

Subjects are then told that the cards below contain information about four people. Each card represents a person. One side of a card tells whether a person accepted the benefit and the other side of the card tells whether that person paid the cost. Finally, the subjects are told to indicate only the card(s) that you definitely need to turn over in order to see whether anyone is breaking the law.

```
benefit
accepted
```

(P)
(Q)

> | benefit *not* accepted |
> | :---: |

(not-P)
(not-Q)

> | cost paid |
> | :---: |

(Q)
(P)

> | cost *not* paid |
> | :---: |

(not-Q)
(not-P)

Cosmides and Tooby wanted to test whether people have internalized conditional rules specifically adapted to detect cheaters: in short, those violating the social contract. Unfortunately, the task used is unable to distinguish between improved performance due to the specially adapted rules in question and improved performance due to the familiarity of the task. In any case, it appears that we cannot simply infer *irrationality* from poor performance on the original, abstract selection task.

Performance improves markedly when subjects are asked to identify violations of conditional rules that express social contracts of familiar and concrete sorts. We can see quite easily, in the case of the Drinking Age Problem, that we must turn over both the *drinking beer* card and the *16 years old* card. About 75 percent of college students choose both of these cards, compared to 25 percent for the abstract version of the selection task. Does the repeatedly poor performance on the abstract version of the task imply that people are irrational? Some have claimed "No." L. J. Cohen (1986) has argued that it is impossible for such experiments to demonstrate irrationality.

Drawing on Noam Chomsky's distinction between competence and performance, Cohen argues that we have an internalized store of rational inference rules, much like the internalized grammar

Chomsky postulates to explain language comprehension and per-formance. Our rationality consists in our *having* those rules, not in our always performing in ways that display rational judgment. If we can make grammatical errors due to inattention and still enjoy grammatical competence, we can certainly violate a rule of inference due to inattention and enjoy rational competence.

Many critics of the Tversky-Kahneman research, such as Gigeren-zer (1991), argue that the errors identified are artifacts of task demands or of the ways questions are formulated. According to this view, cognitive appreciation of relative frequencies becomes diffi-cult when sample size increases, and several of the Tversky-Kahne-man effects apparently trade on this fact. Cohen (1986) contends that the questions are formulated in such a way that subjects are unable to attend to sample size, encouraging them instead to focus on causal considerations. Something like this criticism can be found in Daniel Dennett's reaction to this work as well:

> How rational are we? Recent research in social and cognitive psy-chology (e.g., Tversky and Kahneman 1974; Nisbett and Ross 1980) suggests we are only minimally rational, appallingly ready to leap to conclusions or be swayed by logically irrelevant features of situations, but this jaundiced view is an illusion engendered by the fact that these psychologists are deliberately trying to produce situations that provoke irrational responses — inducing pathology in a system by putting strain on it — and succeeding, being good psychologists. (1987, p. 52)

The experiments demonstrating the biases, however, ask subjects to make judgments of a sort we make routinely. So, it does not look as though subjects need to be specially prepared before they will make similar errors in natural settings. On the contrary, we routinely make such errors unless special attention is devoted to their anticipation and correction. (For more detailed discussions of this literature, see Stich 1990 and Gilovich 1991.)

The key issue concerns what can best explain the apparently irrational cognitive phenomena surveyed. Many theorists hold that such apparent violations of rationality reveal not the disposi-tional frailties of human thought, but the limitations and undue abstractness of the normative rules in question. These theorists add that such "errors" result from situational features of certain tasks. In fact, if the rationality of a judgment depends on specific and sometimes arcane information (and so not on putatively neutral and perfectly general maxims), then rationality depends more on content and context than traditionally supposed. We thus are left with the question of the extent to which such "content and context relativity" leads to relativism in epistemology and the theory of rationality.

INTEGRATIVE CONSIDERATIONS ABOUT RATIONALITY

Rationality serves many masters, many means and ends. The previous example of the Zande witchcraft tradition illustrates that cultures sometimes disagree about the means by which certain functions *should* be served. Individuals in many non-Zande cultures would regard *any* action to be irrational that results from witchcraft beliefs. Others who hold witchcraft beliefs to be false nevertheless may claim that, if such beliefs and practices maintain kinship stability, and kinship stability conduces to the survival of the culture, then it is rational to hold the beliefs and there is no further basis on which to judge the rationality of behavior. Even within our culture, according to some theorists, judgments or patterns of behavior can be rational regardless of whether people are aware of, or could explicitly justify, the means by which an end is achieved or the reasons in virtue of which behavior is rational.

Beyond the substantial difficulties in formulating a general account of rationality (posed, for example, by cultural and social variation), an important theme emerges from the literature we have surveyed: the integrative importance of rationality-bearing factors. The specific conditions for rational inference cannot be plausibly studied independently of systematic investigation of the structure of motivation, the influence of culture, the distribution of (cognitive and economic) resources, and the processing constraints in perception and cognition. This fact recommends a research strategy that unifies perceptual, cognitive, and social factors in human rationality.

Considerations about human rationality bear on epistemology in various ways. Two merit mention here. First, our beliefs can be assessed as either epistemically rational or irrational, relative to their contribution toward (our epistemic goal of) acquiring informative truths and avoiding error. Epistemologists owe us an account of epistemic rationality sensitive to the psychological phenomena outlined in this chapter. Second, the selection of our epistemological standards can be assessed in terms of instrumental rationality, relative to the achievement of our considered epistemic goals. (Perhaps even some nonepistemic goals will figure in the latter assessment.) Chapters 8 and 9 will return to the bearing of instrumental rationality on matters of epistemology.

In sum, then, we have seen that rational assessment is inherently normative, and not merely descriptive. We have also seen that the normative standards for rational assessment can diverge across cultures. This raises questions about the relativity of rationality analogous to our earlier questions about the relativity of truth. Chapter 9 will return to this general topic of relativism in connection with justification. We have also seen that some widely accepted standards of rationality are apparently violated by many people, including many people within our own culture. Regardless of our final judgment on the extent of human irrationality, we have seen that assessments of rationality figure centrally in certain areas of epistemological evaluation. The foregoing cases of apparent irrationality prompt the question whether we should withhold judgment, and thus remain skeptical, about human rationality in certain contexts. We turn, accordingly, to the general topic of skepticism.

8

Skepticism

SOME SPECIES OF SKEPTICISM

We all have doubts about some areas of alleged knowledge, although these doubts will vary among persons and groups. Accordingly, philosophers and others have long debated the limits, or scope, of human knowledge. The more restricted we take the scope to be, the more skeptical we are. So, if we restrict knowledge to claims about our subjective experiences, for example, we are very skeptical indeed. Famous skeptical debates in philosophy have concerned knowledge of, among other things, the mind-independent world, other minds, inductive inferences, historical events, and unobservable entities countenanced by the sciences.

Skepticism, in keeping with most influential philosophical positions, comes in a variety of forms and strengths. Two noteworthy types of skepticism, mentioned briefly in Chapter 1, are *knowledge* skepticism and *justification* skepticism. Unrestricted knowledge skepticism implies that no one knows anything, including this claim itself. Unrestricted justification skepticism implies the more extreme view that no one is even justified in believing anything, including this view itself. We noted, in Chapter 5 that knowledge cannot be undermined by new evidence in the way justification can. For example, if you genuinely know that the moon influences the tides, this knowledge will not be undermined by your acquiring new evidence of any sort. You could thus consistently be skeptical about our having genuine knowledge while granting that we have justification.

Knowledge skepticism in its strongest form implies that it is *impossible*, perhaps even logically impossible, for anyone to know anything. Proponents of such strong skepticism may hold that the essential conditions for our having knowledge make it logically impossible for us to satisfy them. This is a bold skeptical claim, and we know of no argument to substantiate it. A weaker form of knowledge skepticism denies the *actuality* of our having knowledge, but leaves open its possibility. According to this position, we in fact do not know anything, although it may be *possible* for us to have knowledge. Perhaps, for example, our cognitive make-up distorts all our actual input from the world and thus prevents our achieving genuine knowledge. Even so, it would still be possible, in some sense, for us to acquire knowledge, because it would nonetheless be possible for our cognitive make-up to be nondistorting.

Even more moderately, a knowledge skeptic might hold that we simply do not know anything with *certainty*, where certainty is either indubitability (immunity to doubt), infallibility (immunity to error), or irrevisability (immunity to revision). Some philosophers have suggested that our knowledge of mathematical truths enjoys certainty in virtue of having the previous immunities. A skeptic about certainty in all areas would disagree with such philosophers. Knowing with certainty is more demanding than knowledge as justified true belief resistant to the Gettier problem (mentioned in Chapter 5). So, certainty skepticism does not rule out knowledge as ordinarily understood. We could consistently reject knowledge skepticism, and thus justification skepticism, while embracing certainty skepticism. Many philosophers have done so.

Even though skepticism comes in different forms, a common question faces all forms: What status does the skeptical claim itself have? That is, do we *know* that we have no knowledge? Or, are we justified in believing that we have no justified beliefs? Proponents of unrestricted knowledge skepticism will be threatened by a kind of inconsistency if they maintain that they *know* that their skeptical claim is true. They will then be committed both to knowing something and to knowing nothing — an obvious inconsistency. The status of unrestricted knowledge skepticism must, then, be weaker than knowledge. Similarly, proponents of unrestricted justification skepticism will be threatened by inconsistency if they hold that they are justified in believing that their skeptical claim is true. Their position will then imply both that they are justified in believing something and that they are justified in believing nothing. The status of their skeptical thesis must therefore be weaker than justified belief. It may, however, be enough for most skeptics that their claims be *true*, regardless of epistemic status.

Many knowledge skeptics have been limited in their skepticism, being content to dispute only a certain kind of knowledge rather than all knowledge. These skeptics have restricted their skepticism to a particular domain of supposed knowledge: for example, knowledge of the external world, knowledge of other minds, knowledge by induction, knowledge of the past or the future, or knowledge of unperceived items. Restricted skepticism has been more common (if less exciting) than unrestricted skepticism in the history of philosophy, perhaps because it seems more promising in avoiding the aforementioned problem of inconsistency. Of course, all of us are inclined toward skepticism about *something*, or at least we should be, given that far-fetched claims seem ever at hand (certainly as long as tabloid journalism is prominent).

SOME SKEPTICAL ARGUMENTS

Arguments in support of the various species of skepticism are many and diverse. One skeptical argument deserving comment is "the argument from error." This traditional argument assumes that if your present cognitive state (say, a state of believing something about the perceived world) is indistinguishable from another state that does not qualify as knowledge (for example, a state of belief where you were in error, as when you were taken in by a perceptual illusion), then your present state is not actually a state of knowledge.

Descartes presents a version of the argument from error when he questions whether there is any relevant qualitative difference between his waking perceptual states and his dream states. Some skeptics deny that we can identify the relevant difference between the two (and sometimes even that the difference exists), and therefore they claim that we do not have knowledge. For example, if you have no way qualitatively to distinguish your state of believing that there is a computer in the room from your state of believing that there is just a holographic image of a computer in the room, you will be open to the skeptical argument from error. At a minimum, skeptics deserve some kind of answer to their challenge. In the absence of a relevant difference between states of genuine knowledge and states falling short of knowledge, we lose our grip on the very category of genuine knowledge.

One of the most difficult skeptical challenges merits special attention: the Problem of the Criterion. The following version of the problem comes from the sixteenth-century skeptic Michel de Montaigne (1533–1592):

> To adjudicate [between the true and the false] among the appearances of things, we need to have a distinguishing method; to validate this method, we need to have a justifying argument; but to validate this justifying argument, we need the very method at issue. And there we are, going round on the wheel. ([1576], p. 544).

This line of skeptical argument originated in ancient Greece, with epistemology itself. (See Sextus Empiricus, *Outlines of Pyrrhonism,* Book II.)

The argument raises these questions: How can we specify *what* we know (that is, particular cases of knowledge) without having specified *how* we know (for example, how knowledge arises from a reliable source, such as perception). Further, how can we specify *how* we know without having specified *what* we know? It seems that an adequate answer to the question of what we know depends on an understanding of how we know (for example, the relevant reliable sources for our particular cases of knowledge). In addition, it seems that a successful answer to the question of how we know will depend on an understanding of some particular cases of knowledge.

We can approach the problem in terms of a rough analogy. Your identifying a particular animal as a mammal apparently requires your having general standards for when something counts as a mammal. You would use the general standards to distinguish the mammal from the nonmammal. In addition, your having general standards for when something counts as a mammal apparently depends on your having already identified and examined particular cases of mammals (and then inferred the general standards on that basis). Likewise, it seems that an identification of a particular case of knowledge requires your having general standards for when a belief counts as knowledge. In addition, your having general standards for when a belief counts as knowledge apparently depends on your having already identified and examined particular cases of knowledge (and then inferred the general standards on that basis). Is there any plausible way out of this threatening circle?

Contemporary epistemology still lacks a widely accepted reply to the Problem of the Criterion. One influential reply from Roderick Chisholm (1982) rules out skepticism from the start, with the unargued *assumption* that we do know some specific propositions about the external world and can identify these cases of knowledge. Given our previous analogy of mammals, one might react to the threatening circle by simply assuming that one has identified some particular mammals, without relying on an answer to the general question of how it is that we distinguish mammals from nonmammals. Chisholm's approach is called *particularism*, because it begins, not with an answer to general skeptical challenges, but with a positive, nonskeptical answer to the question of what in particular we know. That is, particularism begins with (assumed) *particular* cases of knowledge that we can identify, and uses these to infer answers to general questions of how we know.

A view opposing particularism is called *methodism* (not to be confused with the position of John Wesley's followers). It begins with an answer to the general question of how we know, by specifying the general *methods* by which we acquire knowledge (for example, the methods of ordinary observation and the sciences). Given our analogy of mammals, methodists would react to the threatening circle by assuming that one has general guidelines for distinguishing mammals from nonmammals, even apart from one's having identified some particular mammals. Methodism begins with an answer to the general question of how we know, and then proceeds, on the basis of this answer, to handle questions about particular cases of knowledge.

Some philosophers have faulted particularism for simply assuming what has been questioned by skeptics: that is, what exactly counts as a particular case of knowledge. Particularism seems to assume that some cases of supposed knowledge are cases of genuine knowledge, even though skeptics demand general standards for reasonably holding that any particular case of supposed knowledge is actually a case of genuine knowledge. The analogy: You cannot reasonably assume that something is a mammal in the absence of general standards for distinguishing mammals from nonmammals. Other philosophers have faulted methodism for divorcing knowledge from our considered judgments about particular cases of knowledge. It offers methods, or procedures, of knowing that may not fit with particular instances of supposed knowledge. It also must face questions raised by skeptics about the reliability of proposed methods for knowing. Debates about the Problem of the Criterion are unresolved in contemporary epistemology.

Having identified some species of skepticism and two prominent arguments for skepticism, we turn now to a simple worry that motivates many skeptics. These skeptics raise general questions about the reliability, or the truth conduciveness, of our cognitive sources, such as perception, memory, and introspection. Such skeptical worries might arise from reflection on an actual case of error that was detected but could easily have not been detected. You might believe, for example, that when you were young you broke your arm by falling out of a tree. In a conversation with some older relatives or friends, however, the topic happens to come up and they assure you that you never fell out of a tree but broke your arm in a bicycling accident. You will start to wonder about the reliability of your memory, but you will probably be reassured that your memory can be checked by the testimony of others. You could have similar doubts about perception, if you are sure you heard a baby cry in the next room but your friend assures you that there is only a cat, not a baby, in the next room. Again, you would probably feel reassured that your perception can be checked by the testimony of others or could have been checked by a visual inspection of the room.

Skeptics who raise *general* questions about the reliability, or the truth conduciveness, of our cognitive sources ask about our cognitive sources altogether, that is, *as a whole*. In particular, they ask what convincing reason we have to regard those sources as reliable, as trustworthy for acquiring truth and avoiding error. They would not, therefore, be reassured by having the reliability of one cognitive source (such as an auditory sensation) checked by another cognitive source (such as a visual sensation), because they raise the same skeptical worries about the latter as they raise about the former. It seems that any answer we give to the *general* question of the reliability of our cognitive sources will rely on input from one of the very cognitive sources under question by the skeptic.

One might appeal, for example, to the sensation of touching an apparent computer monitor to test the reliability of a visual experience of an apparent computer monitor. Skeptics will object, however, on the ground that they have asked for a convincing reason to think that touching is reliable as a source of information about the real world. More generally, skeptics have asked for a convincing reason to think that *any* of our cognitive sources is a reliable source of information. So, however broad the diversity of sources invoked (even up to diversity encompassing *all* of our available cognitive sources), skeptics will object, as a result of the generality of their question about reliability of sources. They will not be satisfied by assurances that one cognitive source agrees with any number of other cognitive sources. The problem, in brief, is that we cannot test the reliability of our cognitive sources without relying on them in a way that takes for granted something under dispute by skeptics. (For elaboration of this skeptical worry, see Stroud 1984 and Moser 1993.)

One consideration, according to skeptics, indicates that we will fail to meet the skeptical challenge. Our offering any kind of support for the reliability of our cognitive sources will depend on our use of such cognitive sources as perception, introspection, judgment, memory, testimony, intuition, and common sense. Since all such sources are now being questioned by skeptics, with regard to reliability, our use of them cannot deliver the kind of evidence of reliability sought by skeptics. Unfortunately, we cannot assume a position independent of our own cognitive sources to deliver a test of their reliability of the sort demanded by skeptics. This, for better or worse, is the human cognitive predicament, and no one has yet shown how we can escape it. This consideration suggests that we must take skepticism seriously, especially if we aim to elucidate testing of the reliability of our cognitive sources.

A *pragmatic* defense of our cognitive sources, in terms of their overall utility, will not save the day. Skeptics will ask for convincing reasons to affirm that a belief's overall pragmatic utility is ever a genuinely reliable means of access to how the world really is. It does no good here to note that it is pragmatically useful to regard pragmatic utility as a reliable means to how the world is. A skeptic, once again, seeks reasons free of circularity. Given the aforementioned human cognitive predicament, we can offer little hope for noncircular support on pragmatic grounds. A skeptic demands, but despairs of achieving, noncircular support for beliefs about the reliability of our cognitive sources.

The foregoing skeptical challenges are not necessarily unanswerable, but they do have value in prompting us to reflect on (a) the kind of support we have for our claims to reliable cognitive sources and (b) how we may reasonably proceed in formulating and defending an epistemological theory. Specifically, they prompt us to reflect on whether epistemology may proceed on the basis of intuitions about particular cases of knowledge or on the basis of theoretical considerations about the general nature of knowledge. We shall see later in this chapter that skeptical challenges need not preclude our making claims to knowledge or defending an epistemology, once we acknowledge a central role for explanation in knowledge.

A REPLY FROM COMMON SENSE

A classic challenge to skepticism is found in G. E. Moore's "A Defence of Common Sense" (1925). Moore contends that "the 'Common Sense view of the world' is, in certain fundamental features, *wholly* true" (p. 44). He claims, too, that he knows the relevant common-sense propositions "with certainty." These propositions include the following (1925, p. 33):

1. There now exists a living human that is my body.
2. Before now many human bodies other than mine have lived on earth.
3. The earth had existed for many years before my body was born.
4. I have often perceived my own body and other things that form part of its environment, including other bodies.

Moore also holds that each of us has frequently known, with respect to oneself, the propositions in question. Moore does not specify what feature common to such propositions makes them "common-sense" propositions. He does hold, however, that we know such propositions *with certainty*. Such a "common-sense" approach to knowledge has been very influential in epistemology. We find a version of it in the work of the eighteenth-century philosopher Thomas Reid (1710–1796) and, after Moore, in Roderick Chisholm. Moore's recitation of "common-sense" propositions known with certainty resembles Chisholm's *particularist* approach to knowledge that we mentioned in the previous section.

Moore claims that the common-sense propositions in question find support from a simple consideration. If, according to certain philosophers, no such common-sense proposition is true, then "no philosopher has ever existed, and therefore none can ever have held with regard to any such class [of common-sense propositions] that no proposition belonging to it is true" (p. 40). One's denial of the truth of every such common-sense proposition, according to Moore, entails that one must be wrong in denying this. In short, such a denial lands one in self-refutation.

In reply, skeptics can make two points. First, Moore assumes that if one denies that the common-sense propositions in question are true, then one exists as a living human body. Such denial, according to Moore, requires one's actually being a living human body. What, however, supports this assumption? It is *conceivable* (even if not likely) that we are really disembodied thinking things who do not depend on physical substances for our intellectual lives. Descartes, in the seventeenth century, suggested this possibility in questioning presumed certainty regarding common-sense beliefs. Moore owes us evidence for his assumption that only living human bodies could deny his common-sense propositions.

Second, Moore assumes that we know his common-sense propositions *with certainty*. We can contest this assumption without denying that Moore's common-sense propositions are true. We can deny simply that we know those propositions with certainty, regardless of whether those propositions are true. Whether a proposition is true or false is one issue; whether we know that proposition with certainty, another. You can deny, for example, that you know with certainty that dogs eat lettuce in China. This denial does not require that you deny that it is true that dogs eat lettuce in China. Your denial might be only a disclaimer of supporting evidence for the proposition in question. Moore owes us evidence in support of his assumption that we know his common-sense propositions with certainty.

Moore did hold that he could give a proof of various common-sense propositions in question. In 1939 Moore published his "Proof of an External World," relying on the following claims:

> I can now give a large number of different proofs ["of the existence of things outside of us"], each of which is a perfectly rigorous proof. . . . I can prove now, for instance, that two human hands

exist. How? By holding up my two hands, and saying, as I make a certain gesture with the right hand, "Here is one hand," and adding, as I make a certain gesture with the left, "and here is another." (Pp. 145–46)

Moore claims that his "proof" is "perfectly rigorous," and that it would be "absurd" to suggest that he did not actually know — but merely believed — that there were two hands in the places indicated by his gestures. Such, then, is Moore's "proof" of the existence of external physical objects. Its simplicity is almost breathtaking.

Moore claimed to prove, in addition, that there have been external objects in the past. Thus: "I held up two hands above this desk not very long ago; therefore two hands existed not very long ago; therefore at least two external objects have existed at some time in the past" (1939, p. 148). Moore insists that he does know that he held up two hands in the past, and thus that he has given a "perfectly conclusive proof that external objects have existed in the past."

Moore's position invites an objection. His "proofs" do not give us disproofs of either the claim that he is simply *dreaming* that he is holding up two hands or the claim that he is simply *misremembering* that he held up two hands. Moore's reply is that he cannot prove his claim that here is one hand and there another, but that this is no real problem (1939, p. 149). He finds it adequate that he has "conclusive evidence" for the previous claim, and for the claim that he is not now dreaming or misremembering. We can have, on Moore's view, conclusive evidence for, and certain knowledge of, claims we cannot prove. Moore thus claims to have conclusive evidence that he is not dreaming, even though he cannot tell us what all that evidence is.

In his 1941 paper, "Certainty," Moore considers objections to his claim to certainty that he is not now dreaming. He proposes that "the conjunction of my memories of the immediate past with [present] sensory experiences *may* be sufficient to enable me to know that I am not dreaming" (1941, p. 250). The skeptic's reply will, of course, be that it *is* logically possible that Moore has all his present sensory experiences and memories — even qualitatively characterized — but still is dreaming. Moore counters that "the conjunction of the proposition that I have these sense experiences and memories with the proposition that I am dreaming does seem to me to be very likely self-contradictory" (1941, p. 251). This reply is, however, unconvincing. Moore gives us no reason to suppose it contradictory or inconceivable that he is dreaming while having his present experiences and memories. We have no reason to think that Moore cannot be dreaming while having his present experiences and memories. On the contrary, Moore's dreaming seems perfectly compatible with those experiences and memories. Moore's case for certainty about his common-sense propositions is thus unconvincing.

One might reply that Moore's standards for certainty and conclusiveness fit with our ordinary, nonphilosophical talk of certainty and conclusiveness. Even if there is a merely logical possibility that our bodies do not exist, we typically regard ourselves as knowing with certainty — with conclusive evidence — that our bodies exist. The only *relevant* standards, on this view, are those we typically employ in ordinary, common-sense talk. Since we ordinarily regard our sensory experiences of our bodies as supplying conclusive evidence that we have bodies, we may claim with certainty that we have bodies. A troublesome question from skeptics arises now: How can such an appeal to ordinary standards even begin to engage familiar philosophical questions about the reliability of sensory experience? Skeptical questions such as those of the previous section receive no definite answers from an appeal to ordinary language. Moore's attempts to defend his claims to knowledge seem to be subject to the same skeptical charge of circularity raised in connection with our cognitive sources generally in the previous section.

SKEPTICISM, NATURALISM, AND BROAD EXPLANATIONISM

Some philosophers have tried to avoid the problems of skepticism and traditional epistemology by "naturalizing" epistemology.

A recent naturalist tradition, as Chapter 2 noted, proposes that epistemology be "naturalized" in that it be replaced by the natural sciences. Philosophy, according to the tradition of *replacement naturalism*, is methodologically and doctrinally replaceable by the natural sciences. Epistemology, for instance, is a branch of psychology; it is not a discipline that offers distinctly philosophical standards of assessment for the natural sciences.

Replacement naturalists deny that philosophy is autonomous with respect to the natural sciences. They thus deny that philosophical truths, including truths relevant to epistemology and knowledge, are logically necessary or knowable *a priori*. As a result, according to replacement naturalism, the sciences exhaust epistemology, thereby replacing the philosophical discipline of epistemology. Some other philosophers have offered less austere ways to naturalize philosophy than the way offered by replacement naturalism. We have no objection here to versions of epistemological naturalism other than replacement naturalism. Accordingly, we have no objection to the moderate view that knowledge and justification are natural kinds, that is, kinds of things in the world exemplifying stable properties susceptible to explanation and induction.

A pressing issue for replacement naturalism is: In the absence of any standard independent of the sciences, how are we to discern which of the various sciences are genuinely reliable and thus regulative for purposes of theory formation? (Recall the problems of circularity noted previously in this chapter.) Our list of genuine sciences will likely include the dominant physics and chemistry, but exclude (we hope) astrology and parapsychology. Such a list, regardless of its exact components, seemingly depends on some commitments or standards logically prior to the sciences in question. At any rate, the list arguably depends on some fundamental taxonomic judgments about what the rubric "science" includes. It is an open question, however, whether the judgments in question are analytic or synthetic. (See Chapter 1 on the analytic-synthetic distinction.)

We wish to introduce and recommend a position, called *broad explanationism*, that avoids the problems of replacement naturalism.

(See Chapter 2 for some of those problems.) This kind of explanationism, unlike replacement naturalism, allows that an adequate epistemology depends on commitments that are irreducible to any of the sciences. Broad explanationism permits that good explanation is a general intellectual value, even independently of the sciences. It allows that some good explanations need not be distinctly scientific. More specifically, broad explanationism suggests that our fundamental explanatory goals, represented in part (but not exclusively) by the sciences, should guide how we regulate our beliefs, including our epistemological beliefs concerning what is justified and what unjustified. Some replacement naturalists likewise favor a kind of explanationism, but their version is unduly narrow, restricting the domain of the cognitive and the explanatory to the domain of science (see, for example, Quine 1954, p. 222; 1981, p. 21).

One fundamental twofold goal is to acquire informative truths and avoid falsehoods. Another fundamental goal, for those of us who value the sciences, is to maximize the explanatory value of our belief system with regard to the world and our place in it. That is, we value inference to the best available explanation, or abduction, as a suitable manner of acquiring informative truths and avoiding falsehoods. (On abduction, see Chapter 9.) This agrees with the truth-seeking efforts of the sciences. Such an appeal to our fundamental goals and what we value rests on "instrumental rationality," as characterized in Chapter 7.

Dependence on instrumental rationality is not a feature peculiar to broad explanationism. Even skeptics are guided by their fundamental goals and judgments of value, thereby relying, if only tacitly, on instrumental rationality. In addition, many skeptical arguments owe their force to the value of explaining important epistemological phenomena. Skeptics commonly, if rather tacitly, seem to recommend their skepticism for its explanatory power, for its explanatory superiority over competing epistemological accounts. We note these considerations not to refute skeptics, but rather to signal the pervasive value of best explanation.

Given broad explanationism, we do not have to let skeptical worries about circularity (as in Pyrrhonian skepticism) or the mere possibility of error (as in Cartesian skepticism) control our belief regulation and epistemological positions. We rather can acknowledge that, given our fundamental explanatory goals, skeptics are excessively risk averse. Skeptics purport to err on the side of caution, or error-avoidance, in a way that hinders, from the standpoint of our fundamental values, the acquisition of explanatory truths. Notably, skeptics have not shown that their risk-averse strategy is actually the most effective means to acquiring informative truth and avoiding error. Their risk-aversion manifests a cognitive value commitment that offers no decisive challenge to, or refutation of, broad explanationism. The question of how risk averse one *should* be does not obviously demand an answer favorable to skeptics. Instrumental, goal-directed rationality enables us to hold skepticism at bay, while acknowledging that our preferred "*terra firma*" revolves around our ultimate cognitive goals.

While not favoring unrestricted skepticism, the sciences themselves can, and often do, raise limited skeptical worries and endorse normative standards concerning how beliefs should be regulated. Traditional skeptics often proceed by raising *global* skeptical concerns about the limitations of human knowledge. In contrast, the sciences offer discipline-specific hypotheses that counter, if only by implication, such global skeptical worries. Cognitive psychology, for example, can raise skeptical challenges to parapsychology in virtue of suggesting norms for how belief should be regulated relative to available evidence. In particular, the psychology of statistical inference recommends that generalizations should be sensitive to suitable sample size. Given that the sciences can and do suggest norms of this sort, broad explanationism can likewise acknowledge a role for normative epistemology. It does not have to settle for the mere description of processes of belief formation.

Acknowledging a central (but not exclusive) role for the sciences in explanation and in epistemology fits with the traditional view that epistemology is inherently normative. Even *if* the sciences are largely descriptive, at least at the surface, they are rooted in normative commitments about how beliefs should be formed and regulated. In addition, the sciences are normative in that they make recommendations that delimit research programs by specifying what questions should be pursued. Like the sciences, epistemology is irredeemably normative and, when its goals agree with broad explanationism, it can sidestep many skeptical challenges with a clear conscience.

In sum, then, we have seen that some skeptical challenges, particularly those identifying circularity in our reasoning and testing, merit serious attention from epistemologists. In contrast, challenges stemming from the mere possibility of our being in error fail to threaten claims to knowledge, because knowledge does not require infallible certainty. Skeptical challenges from circularity are more significant. One problem with circularity is that it risks making our reasoning and testing altogether arbitrary, because we can use circular procedures to justify *anything* we like, even obviously irrational positions. Skeptical challenges prompt us to clarify the kinds of reasons we actually have and the kinds of reasons we lack in our claims to knowledge. As a result, we gain better understanding of human knowledge and justification. Skeptical challenges also illustrate the shortcomings of casual reliance on the deliverances of common sense. Recall the defects in Moore's common-sense reply to skepticism. The next chapter will illustrate further the limits on the role of common sense, including common-sense intuitions, in epistemological theory.

9

Epistemology and Explanation

Having identified some of the prominent themes and problems in contemporary epistemology, we do well now to sketch some of their historical origins, with an eye toward standards for resolving those problems. Examining the historical origins of current epistemology will help us to understand more fully the nature of the epistemological problems we have been discussing throughout this book. Once we identify a central problem arising with the emergence of contemporary epistemology—the problem of what exactly has ultimate epistemological authority (for example, common sense, intuitions, or science)—we shall return to the broad explanationism of Chapter 8 to resolve this problem. Our approach will highlight the fact that we as reflective knowers are inherently explainers.

Contemporary Anglo-American epistemology begins with the rebellion of Bertrand Russell (1872–1970) and G. E. Moore (1873–1958) against Kantian and Hegelian idealism at Oxford and Cambridge. F. H. Bradley (1846–1924) and John McTaggart (1866–1925) were two leading proponents of the British idealism challenged by Russell and Moore. Russell reports:

> It was towards the end of 1898 that Moore and I rebelled against both Kant and Hegel. Moore led the way, but I followed closely in his footsteps. I think that the first published account of the new philosophy was Moore's article in *Mind* [1899] on "The Nature of Judgment." Although neither he nor I would now adhere to all the doctrines in this article, I, and I think he, would still agree with its negative part — i.e., with the doctrine that fact is in general independent of experience. (1959, p. 42)

Russell, following Moore, opposed any kind of idealism entailing that "there can be nothing which is not experienced or experience" (1959, p. 107). The view of Russell and Moore that "fact is in general independent of experience [and other mental activity]" entails *realism* about facts. Realism about a fact, F, is just the view that F exists but does not depend for its existence on a conceiver's experiencing, conceiving of, or having a belief about F.

Moore contrasted his realism with Kantian and Hegelian idealism as follows:

> [My] theory . . . differs ["from Kant's theory of perception"] chiefly in substituting for sensations, as the data of knowledge, concepts; and in refusing to regard the relations in which they stand as, in some obscure sense, the work of the mind. It rejects the attempt to explain "the possibility of knowledge," accepting the cognitive relation as an ultimate *datum*. . . . It thus renounces the supposed unity of conception guaranteed by Idealism even in the Kantian form, and still more the boasted reduction of all differences to the harmony of "Absolute Spirit," which marks the Hegelian development. (1899, p. 183)

Moore claimed that a "concept is not a mental fact, nor any part of a mental fact" (1899, p. 179). Concepts, he held, are the only objects of knowledge, and existing things are simply concepts or complexes thereof. (The following remarks about external objects do not depend, however, on the peculiar view that objects are concepts.)

Russell and Moore opposed idealism not only with the ontological claim that there are mind-independent facts, but also with the epistemological claim that they *know* that there are such facts. What, however, was the ground for the latter epistemological claim? Russell explains:

> Bradley argued that everything common sense believes in is mere appearance; we [Moore and Russell] reverted to the opposite extreme, and thought that *everything* is real that common sense, uninfluenced by philosophy or theology, supposes real. With a sense of escaping from prison, we allowed ourselves to think that grass is green, that the sun and stars would exist if no one was aware of them, and also that there is a pluralistic timeless world of Platonic ideas. (1944, p. 12)

The ground, according to Russell, is "common sense, uninfluenced by philosophy or theology." What, however, is common sense? Surprisingly, Russell and Moore do not say in any detail. A plausible, if somewhat vague, interpretation is that common sense for a group of people consists of beliefs common to a wide range of people within that group. Neither Russell nor Moore, however, appeals just to common sense of that sort. Neither argues, for instance, that since most people believe that God exists, we know that God exists.

Russell speaks of common sense *uninfluenced by philosophy or theology*. Why, however, should we regard such common sense as a philosophically adequate ground for challenging idealism and supporting realism? In particular, why should we regard such common sense as a reliable source of *correct* belief regarding idealism and realism? Russell does exclude common sense influenced by philosophy or theology, and thereby invites two troublesome questions.

First, are common-sense beliefs ever altogether uninfluenced by philosophy, given a familiar broad sense of "philosophy"? Don't common-sense beliefs, in other words, typically involve broadly theoretical assumptions that are "philosophical"? Common-sense empirical beliefs about household physical objects, for example, typically rest on subjunctive conditionals. For instance, if I were to drop this glass on the hard floor, it would shatter. Such conditionals are theoretical in that they go beyond simple description of what is currently present in perceptual experience. Russell does not say whether theoretical beliefs of that sort are "philosophical." It is difficult, in any case, to assess Russell's view without a clear statement of what he means by the term "philosophy."

Second, why should we think that common-sense beliefs uninfluenced by philosophy or theology are reliable, or are any more reliable than other common-sense beliefs? Common-sense beliefs influenced by certain kinds of sociology, psychology, politics, or astronomy, for example, can be just as unreliable as common-sense beliefs influenced by certain kinds of philosophy or theology. A widely held belief uninfluenced by philosophy or theology could still be highly unreliable owing to influence from other sources: for example, prejudicial political tactics. Perhaps, then, Russell would appeal to common-sense beliefs uninfluenced by *any* other beliefs. This would perhaps avoid the problem at hand, but only by making it questionable whether there are any common-sense beliefs of the relevant sort. It is unclear, in any case, that any common-sense beliefs are influenced by *no* other beliefs. If there are such common-sense beliefs, they are very rare indeed — too rare to underwrite the rich theoretical work of epistemology and philosophy in general.

A controlling feature of the common-sense theories of Moore and Russell is *empiricism*: the view that the empirical evidence of the senses — for example, visual, auditory, tactile, or gustatory experiences — is a sort of evidence appropriate to genuine knowledge. Russell's empiricism is more explicit than Moore's. Russell claims:

> Nothing can be known to *exist* except by the help of experience. That is to say, if we wish to prove that something of which we have no direct experience exists, we must have among our premises the existence of one or more things of which we have direct experience. Our belief that the Emperor of China exists, for example, rests upon testimony, and testimony consists, in the last analysis of sense-data seen or heard in reading or being spoken to. (1912, pp. 74–75; cf. 1959, pp. 97–98)

Russell sides with such empiricists as Locke, Berkeley, and Hume, against the rationalist view that *a priori* knowledge — knowledge independent of specific experience—can yield knowledge of what actually exists.

Russell sides with such rationalists as Descartes and Leibniz (1646–1716) on the point that logical principles—whether deductive or inductive—are not known on the basis of support from experience. All support from experience, Russell claims, *pre*supposes logical principles. Russell does allow, though, that our knowledge of logical principles is elicited or caused by experience. He thus permits a distinction between the *warrant* and the *cause* of a belief. In sum, Russell holds that "all knowledge which asserts existence is empirical, and the only *a priori* knowledge concerning existence is hypothetical, giving connexions among things that exist or may exist, but not giving actual existence" (1912, p. 75). Russell's empiricism is thus moderate, allowing for some *a priori* knowledge.

Russell's epistemology, unlike Moore's, attributes definite epistemological significance to the natural sciences—a significance that gives the sciences an epistemological priority over common sense. (This is especially true of Russell's epistemological views after 1918.) Russell acknowledges that the sciences begin with common-sense notions and judgments: for example, notions of causation, space, time, and things. The sciences, however, often need to revise or to eliminate such common notions to achieve their explanatory purposes. Russell observes that we typically start our theorizing from "naive realism," the view that things are as they seem. We initially think that the objects we perceive really are as they appear: that snow is white, that fire is hot, that feathers are soft, and so on. The natural sciences, however, offer a strikingly different view of the objects we perceive—a view entailing that the features ascribed to external objects by naive realism do not really inhere in the external objects themselves. Russell thus remarks that "naive realism leads to physics, and physics, if true, shows that naive realism is false" (1940, p. 15).

Philosophy, according to Russell, serves an important purpose here: It identifies how fundamental common-sense notions might be reconstructed to benefit the explanatory aims of the sciences. Russell denies, however, that philosophy offers a kind of knowledge ultimately different from scientific knowledge. He holds that "philosophy involves a criticism of scientific knowledge, not from a point of view ultimately different from that of science, but from a point of view less concerned with details and more concerned with the harmony of the whole body of special sciences" (1927, p. 2).

ULTIMATE EPISTEMOLOGICAL AUTHORITY

Why should we take science as our ultimate epistemological authority? This question will be especially pressing for those inclined toward skepticism about the reliability of science. Surprisingly, Russell offers little by way of reply:

> For my part, I assume that science is broadly speaking true. . . . But against the thoroughgoing sceptic I can advance no argument except that I do not believe him to be sincere. (1950, p. 382)

This reply will probably convince nobody. Russell understands the *truth* of statements as their describing *facts* that may be objective in that they transcend experience (1948, pp. 149, 151; 1940, chaps. 16–17). He gives no reason, however, for thinking that everyone doubtful of science's delivering such truth is insincere.

Epistemologists have long debated whether perception, memory, and the procedures of the natural sciences deliver objective truths. We cannot convincingly settle this debate by assuming that beliefs based on perception, memory, or the sciences are broadly true, and that people doubting this assumption are insincere. The use of the latter assumption (if we may borrow a famous phrase from Russell) aims to secure by theft what will be secured, if at all, only by extensive philosophical toil.

Skeptics will object not only to unjustified appeals to the reliability of the sciences, but also to appeals to "preanalytic epistemic data" as a basis for justifying epistemological claims. The latter appeals have attracted many philosophers in the phenomenological tradition of Franz Brentano (1838–1917) and Edmund Husserl (1859–1938) and many philosophers in the common-sense tradition of Reid, Moore, and Chisholm. The rough idea is that we have pretheoretical access, via "intuition" or "common sense," to certain considerations about justification, and these considerations can support one epistemological view over others.

It is rather unclear what the epistemic status of the relevant preanalytic epistemic data is supposed to be. Such data, we often hear, are accessed by "intuitions" or by "common sense." We thus hear some epistemologists talk as follows: "Intuitively (or commonsensically) justification resides in a particular case like *this*, and does not reside in a case like *that*." A statement of this sort aims to guide our formulation of a notion of justification or at least a general explanatory principle concerning justification. A simple question arises: Is such a statement *self*-justifying, with no need of independent epistemic support? If so, what notion of self-justification can sanction the deliverances of intuition or common sense, but exclude spontaneous judgments no better, epistemically, than mere prejudice or guesswork?

Literal talk of self-justification evidently admits, quite implausibly, unrestricted justification. If one statement can literally justify itself, *solely in virtue of itself*, then *every* statement can. Statements do not differ on their supporting themselves: For any statement *P*, *P* guarantees *P*. Such "support" is universal. A widely accepted adequacy condition on standards of justification is, however, that they not allow for the justification of *every* proposition, that they not leave us with an "anything goes" approach to justification. Literal self-justification runs afoul of this condition. Some philosophers apparently use the term "self-justification" in a *non*literal sense, but we need not pursue this interpretive matter here.

Intuitive judgments and common-sense judgments can, and sometimes do, result from special, even biased, linguistic training. Why then should we regard such judgments as *automatically* epistemically authoritative? Apparently we should not. Intuitive judgments and common-sense judgments certainly can be false, as but a little reflection will illustrate. Such judgments, furthermore, seem not always to be supported by best available evidence. Consider, for instance, how various judgments of "common sense" are at odds with our best available evidence from the natural sciences. It is unclear, then, why we should regard intuitive judgments or common-sense judgments as the basis of any of our standards for justification.

Perhaps, as the anthropologist Clifford Geertz suggests, we should not regard common sense as a reliable faculty or source for our judgments:

> Common sense is not a fortunate faculty, like perfect pitch; it is a special frame of mind, like piety or legalism. And like piety or legalism (or ethics or cosmology), it both differs from one place to the next and takes, nevertheless, a characteristic form. (Geertz 1983, p. 11; cf. chap. 4)

We have, in any case, no straightforward answer to the question why we should regard the judgments of common sense or intuition as epistemically authoritative.

A directly analogous question confronts an appeal to our "ordinary use" of the term "justification" as the basis for explaining and arguing for justification. If you are a contextualist, for example, you might try to justify your position by appeal to this statement: We ordinarily use the term "justification" in accord with contextualist assumptions. (See Malcolm 1942 for an appeal to ordinary language for such epistemological purposes.)

An appeal to ordinary language-use raises problems on at least two counts. First, there is troublesome vagueness in the phrase "our ordinary use." What determines *ordinary* use? In particular, *who* exactly are the relevant language-users? It is doubtful that straightforward answers are forthcoming. Ordinariness of use, in any case, seems context relative and subject to variation. Second, it is unclear why we should think that ordinary language use favorable to contextualism is sufficient to *justify* contextualism in a manner appropriate to knowledge. It seems quite conceivable that ordinary language-use is *un*justified under certain circumstances; it certainly is unreliable in some cases.

The problem at hand concerns what, if anything, is ultimately authoritative in epistemology: intuitions (say, of common sense) or theory (say, scientific theory)? We shall sketch a position that reconciles intuitions and theory while acknowledging a central role for best available explanation in knowledge. This will be in keeping with the broad explanationism introduced in Chapter 8. Let us turn, then, to the role of explanation in knowledge.

EXPLANATION AND KNOWLEDGE

Explanation figures prominently in the philosophical study of knowledge, partly because it is involved in a widespread species of epistemic justification and knowledge. We shall briefly examine the distinctive character of explanatory knowledge and the ways in which our attempts to find explanations influence what statements we should accept as true, including the claims of epistemology.

Explanatory Knowledge

Let's first clarify to some extent what explanatory knowledge is. Explanatory knowledge is usually contrasted with descriptive knowledge. Descriptive knowledge is characterized by Aristotle as *knowledge that* something is the case, whereas explanatory knowledge is *knowledge why* something is the case. Explanation is therefore also described as an answer to a certain type of why question (although some why questions call not for an explanation but for an epistemic justification). For example, you can know *that* your friend Fred winces noticeably every time he hears the expression "freezer burn" without having any idea *why* he behaves in this way. You have descriptive knowledge of how he behaves but lack explanatory knowledge of why he behaves this way.

It is common to require that explanatory knowledge be true, or factual. Pre-Copernican astronomers thought they had descriptive knowledge that the planets sometimes appear to move backward relative to their normal course against the background of the fixed stars. They also thought they had explanatory knowledge of why this retrograde motion occurs. It turns out that their Ptolemaic "explanation" was wrong. So, we would say that they did not really possess (explanatory) knowledge of why this retrograde motion occurs. We can use the term "potential explanation" for knowledge that seems to be explanatory but turns out not to be correct.

Explanatory knowledge differs from descriptive knowledge, but it should not be completely separated from descriptive knowledge. Explanation is a *type* of descriptive knowledge; so it falls under the heading of propositional knowledge generally. If you explain why Fred winces when he hears "freezer burn," you will do so by supplying additional descriptive knowledge of the situation. You might say something to the effect of "He once had a very bad experience with freezer burn." Whatever the explanation is, it will be conveyed through a certain body of information in descriptive claims about the situation. So explanatory knowledge is descriptive knowledge of a particular sort. Not all descriptive knowledge is explanatory, as we have seen, but all explanatory knowledge consists of descriptive claims.

Our characterization of explanatory knowledge presents a problem. How should we identify the species of propositional knowledge that is explanatory? What is it about some propositional knowledge that makes it explanatory? Philosophers have put forward various theories of explanation to answer these questions. We shall present a few of the most influential claims about the nature of explanation. This will illuminate our talk of explanatory knowledge.

One of the most common ideas is that explanatory knowledge is knowledge of certain propositions that make up an *argument.* The claim that needs to be explained, called the *explanandum,* is the conclusion of the argument, and the explaining propositions are the premises of the argument. On this view, an explanation provides descriptive knowledge that would have led one rationally to *expect* the explanandum if one had possessed that knowledge before the event occurred. The argument can be either deductive or inductive, but it must present information that would justify belief in the occurrence of the explanandum if one had no prior knowledge of its occurrence. The comments about Fred's bad experience with freezer burn could be part of an argument supporting the explanandum. If we add some general claims about how people tend to experience pain when they are reminded of a bad experience and about how people often wince as a sign of feeling some internal pain, we have at least a sketch of an argument that would lead one to have expected Fred to wince when he hears "freezer burn."

Some of Aristotle's comments on explanatory knowledge suggest that explanation is argument. A similar view has been developed and defended more recently by Carl Hempel (1965). According to this position, explanatory knowledge is similar in structure to predictive knowledge. If you know, for example, that being reminded of a bad experience tends to cause internal pain and that the experience of internal pain tends to cause behavior like wincing or making a pained facial expression, and if you know that Fred once had a bad experience with freezer burn, you can *predict* his wincing, or something like it, even if you have never seen him react in this way. Explanation, according to this theory, is like predicting an event *after the fact.* After the occurrence of the explanandum, information that *would have* allowed us to predict the event serves to explain the event. This information comes in the form of an argument supporting the assertion that the explanandum occurs.

The foregoing theory of explanation has intuitive appeal but raises some difficulties. Some explanations, it seems, do not present information that could have supported a prediction of the explanandum before it occurred. They do not show the explanandum to have been likely to occur given the initial conditions. One commonly discussed example from medicine is the explanation of paresis (a slight paralysis) in a patient who has syphilis. One does not get paresis unless one already has syphilis, but only a small percentage of people with syphilis contract paresis. Knowing that someone has syphilis does not allow you to *predict* that he will get paresis, but if you see that he gets paresis you can explain it by citing his syphilis. The syphilis explains the paresis although it cannot support a prediction of paresis.

Another problem with the argument view of explanation is that some information is predictive without being explanatory. You might have seen Fred wince many times in the past whenever he hears "freezer burn," and that would support a prediction that he will wince the next time he hears the dreaded phrase. This experience of a pattern in his behavior does not, however, explain his behavior. In fact, this general pattern in his behavior is just what needs to be explained.

Responding to problems with the theory of explanations as arguments, philosophers have recently emphasized that many explanations rely on claims about *causation*. Some information can allow us to predict an event, but if it does not identify a cause of the event, it will not be explanatory. Further, some causes do not support predictions of their effects. Syphilis is a cause (at least in the sense that it is a salient necessary condition) of paresis. So, syphilis can explain the occurrence of paresis, but it does not guarantee or even make likely the occurrence of paresis and hence cannot predict paresis. The distinguishing feature of explanations, on this view, is that they supply descriptive knowledge of the causes of the events we want to explain. Explanations are a special kind of description of the situation, and what makes them special is that they describe the *relevant causes* of the explanandum.

Of course, not all explanations are causal. Explanations in mathematics and logic, for example, are not causal. In addition, some explanations concern only *how* things function without specifying what causes them to function as they do. For example, the instructions for your new computer might explain how, in practical terms, its multimedia system functions without identifying why it functions as it does. The instructions would thus offer a noncausal explanation. Nonetheless, many explanations do identify causes, and explanatory knowledge often depends on knowledge of causal connections. An adequate theory of explanation will therefore involve a theory of causation.

Perhaps our beliefs that various external (that is, mind-independent) physical objects exist offer causal explanations of our richly diversified but remarkably stable perceptual experiences of apparent physical objects. For example, your belief that there is a book before you may explain why you are now having a visual experience and a tactile experience of an apparent book. This belief may explain your experiences in virtue of its answering the question of why you are having your current visual and tactile perceptual experiences. Its answer acknowledges the existence of a mind-independent physical object (a book) that makes sense of, partly in virtue of unifying, your current experiences. Many scientific beliefs (including beliefs about electrons and quarks) offer similar unifying causal explanations, even if their causal explanations are probabilistic rather than deterministic.

Inference to the Best Explanation

Much of our knowledge of the world is based on considerations of the *explanatory power* of various claims about the world. We often justifiably accept a belief about something because it offers the best available explanation of some aspect of our experience that seems to need an explanation. This type of justification for a belief is called "inference to the best explanation," because it infers from some data a proposition that provides the best available explanation of the data. It is also called "abductive inference." This sort of inference to an explanatory hypothesis is especially important in the sciences whenever we infer the existence of some unobservable entity, such as subatomic particles, to explain the observable outcomes of experiments.

A standard example of abductive inference comes from astronomy. Early in the last century, astronomers knew of the existence of only seven planets: Mercury, Venus, Earth, Mars, Jupiter, Saturn, and Uranus. They observed that the orbit of Uranus was not exactly what it should be according to their calculations. This was something that needed to be explained. In addition, they felt the need to explain it because it was unexpected. They reasoned that if there were an as-yet-unobserved eighth planet beyond Uranus, the gravitational effect of that eighth planet on Uranus would nicely explain the orbit they actually observed. They postulated that such a planet exists, and eventually they observed it through powerful telescopes right where it was expected to be. The eighth planet was Neptune. This episode from the history of astronomy presents a clear example of a (successful) inference to the best explanation.

We noted, at the beginning of this chapter, a dispute involving realism and idealism treated by Russell and Moore. The principle of inference to the best explanation may enable us to resolve this dispute. Consider, again, our belief that various external physical objects exist—say, such household objects as chairs, tables, and computers. Each of us has a wide range of diverse but stable experiences of such apparent objects, including visual, tactile, and auditory experiences. What offers the best explanation of this range of experiences? Our broad explanationism, introduced in Chapter 8, proposes that the best explanation comes from our familiar beliefs that the relevant household physical objects actually exist, that is, exist independently of our beliefs that they exist.

Idealists who deny the objective existence of the household physical objects in question will be hard put to answer what best explains our wide range of experiences of such apparent objects. It is noteworthy that we have no indication whatever of our typically "calling up imaginary images" of such objects. So, we may be duly suspicious of any explanatory hypothesis implying that in ordinary experience we are simply calling up imaginary images. This is not a refutation of idealism. It rather is a point that shifts a heavy explanatory burden to idealists. We find that realism about physical objects offers the best means of discharging that burden. Its being the best means derives from its supplying the most fitting account of our range of perceptual experiences. Many philosophers find that a strategy of inference to best explanation can resolve philosophical problems concerning, for example, other minds, historical knowledge, scientific unobservables, and knowledge by induction.

One difficulty with inference to the best explanation is that our *intuitions* about what counts as the best explanation of something are variable. Our intuitions may be theory dependent in that they can be shaped by our prior beliefs about the nature of the world, specifically about the nature of causation. Our judgments about explanation will be constrained by what we believe exists in the world to operate as a causal agent, what types of causal interaction occur in the world, and so forth. For example, a person who believes in some instances of teleological explanation will be able to support explanatory inferences that a person who rejects teleological explanation will not. (Teleological explanation proceeds by citing goals or purposes.) There will also be significant differences between people who accept probabilistic causal relationships and those who accept only deterministic causal relationships.

The variability in notions of explanation threatens to present a dangerous kind of relativity in our knowledge claims, if explanation is as important for knowledge as we have suggested. To avoid an "anything goes" approach to explanatory knowledge, we must find some way rationally to constrain what counts as an explanation and what counts as a *better* explanation than some other explanation. That is, we need further clarification of the nature of explanation itself. Until we have a complete and satisfactory theory of explanation, our knowledge by inference to the best explanation will be somewhat problematic.

The problematic nature of explanatory knowledge is not a minor flaw in our overall epistemology, to be worked out whenever we get around to it. Rather, it has major significance for our entire epistemology, our entire understanding of ourselves as *knowers*. This is because it seems that all our knowledge is dependent in some ways on central explanatory hypotheses we accept about the world and ourselves. The key explanatory hypothesis of naturalism, for example, will shape all of the explanatory inferences naturalists make about the specific character of the world, including themselves. It will have a profound influence on the naturalist's entire quest for knowledge. Acceptance of some competing central explanatory hypothesis will direct one's entire quest for knowledge in other directions. What we need is some rational way to choose between competing central explanatory hypotheses about the world, say, realism and idealism about perceptual objects.

The problem of how rationally to select from among competing explanatory hypotheses at a very basic, metaphysical level presents unique challenges. Rationality is often determined only relative to some basic worldview, or ontology. Specification of rational or justified belief often presupposes a basic metaphysical framework. The challenge in justifying basic metaphysical claims is that we have no further, more fundamental metaphysical assumptions to draw from.

There are some widely accepted constraints on acceptable explanation. Most philosophers believe that *ad hoc explanation,* for example, is generally unacceptable. An ad hoc explanation is an explanation introduced specifically for the purpose of saving some favored theory from apparent disconfirmation. For example, some proponents of the flat-earth hypothesis postulate a NASA conspiracy to try to account for the available photos of the spherical earth. In a similarly ad hoc manner, some psychics explain failed demonstrations of their power in terms of interference from nonbelievers' negative psychic energy. If a proposed explanation lacks any independent motivation or justification, it has been introduced in an inappropriate way, and hence should not be accepted.

Another generally accepted restriction on explanation is known as Ockham's razor. This is the principle that explanations should not postulate different kinds of entities any more than is *necessary* for adequate explanation of the available data. Although there are such widely accepted general constraints on acceptable explanation, there remains a significant degree of variability in notions of explanation at a more specific level.

The best candidate for justifying a deep explanatory hypothesis about the nature of the world is a set of fundamental intellectual values, most notably the fundamental twofold value of acquiring significant, explanatory truths and avoiding error. If objectivity is built into our *definition* of "truth" (see Chapter 4), this will carry over to more specific objective constraints on what can count as explanation and what counts as a better explanation than some other. When we infer to an explanatory hypothesis, we do not seek only an elegant explanation, regardless of its empirical consequences. If our only objective were to tell a good story that has some explanatory character to it, we would generate many of the problems of relativism.

The intellectual goal to have an explanatory story is balanced against the goal of acquiring truth and avoiding error. Unless our *definition* of truth is relativistic, we can avoid an "anything goes" approach to explanation and abductive inference by requiring that abductive inference lead us to significant truths. Our explanatory theories, more specifically, must answer to the relevant *evidence*, and mere belief in a statement does not count as evidence. Perceptual experience, for example, must support our empirical theories, and such experience is not a matter of mere belief: it is, after all, *perceptual*. For example, our range of experiences of apparent physical objects is not a matter of our mere beliefs. Such experiences, as noted in Chapter 5, often arise *prior to* our forming any beliefs about them. We have seen that this consideration figures in the isolation objection to coherence theories of justification. Our perceptual experiences call for explanation, and in doing so, can place definite constraints on what propositions are epistemically justified in virtue of supplying a best explanation of relevant data.

Some philosophers disagree about how abductive inference relates to other forms of inductive inference, such as "induction by simple enumeration." Induction by simple enumeration, as suggested in Chapter 7, starts with a number of particular examples and generalizes from them. For example, if you observe enough cases of Fred wincing when he hears "freezer burn," you will infer the general claim that he always winces when he hears "freezer burn." As we've seen, this does not automatically explain his behavior, but some philosophers have argued that some inference to the best available explanation underwrites every inference by enumeration. We must appeal to explanation, these philosophers claim, to justify the conclusion on the basis of the premises.

Our inference (that Fred always winces when he hears "freezer burn") assumes that Fred does not behave this way *only* when we are present. It assumes that what we have observed is a *representative* sample of Fred's behavior, and this assumption can be justified only with the claim that it is the best available explanation of how we came to possess the evidence we possess. Specifically, the enumerative inference is based on the inference that a *general regularity* in Fred's behavior is a better explanation of what we've observed than the claim that Fred behaves this way *only* when we are present. Given all our background information, the hypothesis that Fred is just acting this way for us is a gratuitous explanatory hypothesis, and the hypothesis that we are seeing instances of a general regularity is a much more natural explanation.

Other philosophers have argued that abductive inference reduces to ordinary enumerative induction in combination with other familiar forms of inference. The claim here would be that we infer a general regularity behind the observed behavior as the result of an inductive generalization from cases in the past in which we have found observed regularities to indicate general patterns. We may have often found in the past that when we observe some pattern of behavior in other persons it is the result of a genuine, widespread regularity in their behavior rather than a peculiar behavior unique to certain circumstances. In other words, our identification of the best available explanation for what we've observed is determined, on this view, by simple inductive generalization from similar situations we've been in before.

Abductive inference is clearly closely linked to other forms of inductive inference and even to deductive inference, although it is unclear whether it can be reduced to other forms of inference. Even if it can be reduced, it is worth identifying it as a distinct form of inference because of the explicit appeals it makes to explanation. Many inferences make no such explicit appeals to explanation. The study of abduction, therefore, highlights the central importance of explanatory hypotheses in our knowledge of the world, including knowledge of ourselves and other people as knowers.

Explainers, Understanding, and Epistemological Authority

We seek knowledge, not in an unstructured pursuit of any random piece of information, but always within a structured overall pursuit of *significant* truths. Some knowledge is obviously more important than other knowledge, because of its explanatory power, its connections to other pieces of knowledge, its utility, and the insight into the world that it affords. We suspect that few people have as a fundamental intellectual goal the justified belief in and retention of all true propositions they happen to come across. Such a goal would be appropriate only for one pursuing a championship title in *Trivial Pursuit*. (Actually, the facts one needs to know in *Trivial Pursuit* are highly selective for their historical and cultural significance. The unstructured pursuit of knowledge we are assessing would be appropriate for a much *more trivial* version of *Trivial Pursuit.*)

Our point is that human knowers are primarily *theorizers* rather than simple fact-gatherers. One can find evidence for this in the earliest recorded human history. We theorize about each other, in order to understand what makes us tick, to explain why people behave as they do. We theorize about the natural world around us, to understand how it works, to explain why natural events occur. One might prefer to emphasize another important goal: the ability to predict and control our environment. At a practical level, this is perhaps our basic value. We constantly strive to control our environment for the sake of survival and prosperity. At an intellectual level, however, our fundamental goal is *understanding*. Like ourselves, the Azande mentioned in Chapter 7 seek understanding of their environment, even if their theories and methods differ from ours. It is highly unsatisfying to have the kind of knowledge that enables us to predict and control our environment if we lack the kind of explanatory knowledge that allows us to understand our environment (and ourselves). As a result, we have become theorizers *par excellence*.

Explanation provides a basic motivation not only for the pursuit of knowledge, but also for the philosophical study of knowledge, which is itself the pursuit of a certain kind of knowledge. Epistemology itself is very much a quest for explanations, explanations of ourselves *as knowers*. Many of the theoretical debates in epistemology are debates about what counts as the best explanation of some aspect of our epistemic nature. Epistemology itself is hence subject to a higher level evaluation, a *meta-epistemology*. How one resolves debates within epistemology and how one understands the project of epistemology depend very much on one's views on the nature of explanation. They presuppose some set of intellectual values in the service of which we engage in knowledge-seeking activity.

In keeping with our broad explanationism, we propose using a basic concern for explanatory power and explanatory coherence, relative to our total evidence, as a way of resolving the problem of ultimate epistemological authority. In debates about whether ultimate epistemological authority resides in some privileged set of intuitions, such as those of "common sense," or in some privileged theory, say from science or from metaphysics, we should look for a resolution from considerations of what provides the greatest overall explanatorily satisfactory worldview. We can tolerate a method that sometimes gives more argumentative weight to intuitions, or considered judgments, and sometimes gives more weight to broad theoretical virtues, if this method is guided by a consistent pursuit of some more basic explanatory goal. Skeptical problems, for example, should bother us only if they threaten to undermine an otherwise powerful explanatory hypothesis. If, however, they appear to be excessively risk averse relative to the goal of acquiring explanatory truths, they will not bother us.

The key standard in meta-epistemology is the maximal explanatory coherence of our theories relative to *all* the available evidence, including the data of experience and considered judgments about particular cases of knowledge. Sometimes consideration of all available evidence counsels that nothing can be reasonably concluded, by way of affirmation or denial, about some topic. In such cases, a wait-and-see attitude is advisable. Although there will be some relativity of considered judgments, or intuitions, about particular cases of knowledge, the requirement that we explain the data of experience will keep us from objectionable forms of relativism. It will prevent our explanations from being mere fairy tales, and it will prevent the isolation problem for epistemic coherentism mentioned in Chapter 5. Accordingly, in noting the best explanation provided by our beliefs that physical objects exist, we appealed to the best explanation of our wide range of *perceptual experiences*. These experiences, we have noted, are not themselves beliefs, as they can arise prior to the formation of beliefs.

Although philosophers disagree about what constitutes available evidence, they agree fairly widely that *mere* belief does not qualify as evidence. The only relativity we must accept, it seems, derives from the relativity of instrumental rationality (see Chapters 7 and 8) resulting from the variability in our intellectual goals. This is a relativity that most people should be able to accept—

and perhaps must accept. The objectivity of knowledge and justification is secure, contrary to the relativist, so long as knowledge and justification are natural kinds, and we see no reason to deny that they are.

Broad explanationism, we hold, can itself be justified on explanatory grounds. That is, it offers the best explanation of what we seek in epistemic evaluation: a certain kind of instrumental rationality involving the twofold cognitive goal of achieving significant truth and avoiding error. It thus meets its own standard for justification, and this is more than we can say for some other theories, including certain versions of extreme skepticism. A key reason why we use inference to the best explanation is that, if we didn't, we could not satisfy our avowed explanatory aims. That is, we could not achieve appropriate instrumental rationality involving the twofold cognitive goal of achieving significant truth and avoiding error. So, our recommended methodology is, as philosophers sometimes say, reflexive; the methodological directive we support applies to the directive itself. We are not endorsing a circular argument for our position; we rather are noting one of its logical virtues.

Finally, then, our intuitions are significant in epistemology because we try to explain them. They do not, however, have ultimate epistemological authority, because they are defeasible in light of broader theoretical concerns. The same applies to the considered judgments of common sense. Our preferred background theories have considerable weight in epistemology, because we seek to maintain the explanatory power and coherence of our current worldview. These theories are fallible, however, and can reasonably be rejected in light of deeper explanatory goals. This interplay between intuitions and theory constrained by fundamental explanatory goals fits with the broad explanationism we have introduced. It also subsumes epistemological theorizing under a model for *theorizing in general*, a model recognizing abduction as a central method for gathering knowledge of the world. An adequate epistemology must likewise accommodate our fundamental intellectual goals. For better or worse, we as reflective knowers are explainers—and irredeemably so.

Glossary

A posteriori knowledge: Knowledge that depends on a specific sensory or perceptual experience. Scientific knowledge, according to many philosophers, is a paradigmatic case of *a posteriori* knowledge.

A priori knowledge: Knowledge that does not depend on any specific sensory or perceptual experience. Mathematical knowledge, according to many philosophers, is a paradigmatic case of *a priori* knowledge.

Abduction: Inductive inference to a best (available) explanation; the selection (and justification) of an hypothesis on the basis of its offering an optimal explanation of the relevant data. (See Chapter 9.)

Analytic truth: A statement that is true just in virtue of the meanings of its constituent terms. A standard textbook example is: "All bachelors are unmarried men."

Belief: A representational psychological state related to a proposition. Evidence that an individual is in a belief state can be found in a tendency or disposition to assent to a sentence asserting that proposition under certain circumstances. (See Chapter 3.)

Certainty: May be psychological or epistemic; if psychological, an attitude of full confidence toward a proposition; if epistemic, a special immunity of a proposition, such as infallibility or indubitability.

Coherence: A special kind of interconnectedness relation, such as a logical, probabilistic, or explanatory relation, among propositions. A coherence theory of *truth* defines truth in terms of coherence among propositions in a special set. A coherence theory of *justification* defines justification in terms of coherence among propositions in a special set.

Conditions of knowledge: Essential features, or defining traits, of knowledge, such as belief, truth, and justification.

Content, propositional: The representational information, whether true or false, indicated by "that clauses" in English: that something is the case. Declarative sentences express propositions, and beliefs have propositions as their objects.

Contingent truth: A truth that is not necessarily true, that could have failed to be true if the world had been different. For example, it could have been false (even though it is contingently true) that you are reading this glossary.

Criterion, the problem of: The skeptical challenge to explain the relation between individual cases of what we know and our general guidelines for discerning how we know. (See Chapter 8.)

Deduction: A logically valid form of inference where, necessarily, if the relevant premises are true, then the conclusion is true too. Deduction thus disallows true premises and a false conclusion in an inference.

Defeasibility: The feature of justification in virtue of which it is susceptible to being undermined by the addition of new evidence.

Deontological: Having to do with obligation, or duty. In English, use of "ought" and "should" is typically deontological, signifying an obligation.

Dogmatism: An attitude of refusing to admit the real possibility of error in cases in which such an attitude is ill-founded; holding a position come what may, in the absence of appropriately strong supporting evidence.

Doubt: A psychological attitude of refraining from or suspending belief.

Eliminativism: An extreme form of materialism recommending the elimination of certain vocabulary (e.g., mentalistic vocabulary) or disciplines (e.g., traditional "folk" psychology or epistemology).

Empiricism: The view that the evidence of the senses — e.g., visual, auditory, tactile, olfactory, or gustatory experiences — is a sort of evidence appropriate to genuine knowledge. (*Strict* empiricism: the view that *only* the evidence of the senses is appropriate to genuine knowledge.) (See Chapter 6.)

Epistemic coherentism: The view that all justification is inferential or systematic in virtue of interconnectedness relations among beliefs. (See Chapter 5.)

Epistemic contextualism: The view that justification has a two-tier structure in that some beliefs are "contextually basic"—i.e., taken for granted in a context of inquiry—and all inferentially justified beliefs depend on such contextually basic beliefs. (See Chapter 5.)

Epistemic foundationalism: The view that justification has a two-tier structure in that some instances of justification are noninferential, or foundational, and all other instances of justification are inferential, deriving ultimately from foundational justification. (See Chapter 5.)

Epistemic holism: See *Epistemic Coherentism.*

Epistemic infinitism: The view that regresses of inferential epistemic justification are endless, or infinite. (See Chapter 5.)

Epistemic justification: The kind of warrant or evidence indicative, perhaps probabilistically, of truth and required by propositional knowledge. (See Chapter 5.)

Epistemology: The theory of knowledge, or the philosophical study of the essential conditions, sources, and limits of knowledge.

Explanandum: The thing (e.g., the event, fact, or proposition) being explained in an explanation. A proposition that explains is called an *explanans.*

Explanation: An answer to a certain kind of why question that can provide understanding of some fact or event. (See Chapter 9.)

Explanationism: The epistemological view that epistemic justification should be understood in terms of abductive inference, even if such inference is not consciously deployed or its premises are not accessible to consciousness. (See *Abduction* and Chapter 8.)

Externalism: The view that the epistemic justification for a belief need not be in any way consciously accessible to the believer and that relevant justifying factors can lie outside the believer.

Fallibilism: The view that epistemic justification, for contingent propositions, does not guarantee truth; a contingent belief can be justified for a believer but be false.

Gettier problem: The problem of finding a modification of, or an alternative to, the standard justified-true-belief analysis of knowledge that avoids difficulties from counter-examples to that analysis either presented by or inspired by Edmund Gettier. (See Chapter 5.)

Idealism: The view that the existence of some thing or class of things depends on a conceiver's experiencing, conceiving of, or having a belief about that thing or class of things; one version, associated with George Berkeley, states that "to be is to be perceived."

Induction: Nondeductive, probabilistic inference; in an inductively valid form of inference, if the relevant premises are true, then the conclusion is at least more likely to be true than false. Induction thus allows true premises and a false conclusion in an inference but disallows true premises and a conclusion likely to be false. (See Chapter 6.)

Inference to the best explanation: See *Abduction.*

Inferential justification: The justification of one belief depending on another belief or set of beliefs; inferential justification can be either deductive or inductive. (See Chapter 5.)

Innate knowledge: Knowledge that is inborn, or unlearned, as contrasted with knowledge that is acquired through experience. (See Chapter 6.)

Intentionality: The property of "aboutness" or "directedness" possessed by mental attitudes such as beliefs, desires, and fears; a belief intends an object or state of affairs if it is a belief about that object or state of affairs.

Internalism: The view that epistemic justification for a belief must be consciously accessible to the cognizer, or that the conditions for justification must in some other way be "internal" to the subject.

Introspection: A mental process whereby one becomes aware of some of one's own mental contents.

Intuitions: Spontaneous judgments about what is or must be the case; they are regarded by many philosophers as pretheoretical constraints on theorizing, whether in epistemology or elsewhere in philosophy.

Isolation objection: The objection to epistemic coherentism that it allows for empirically justified beliefs that either contradict, or are improbable given, one's full range of empirical evidence, including nonbelief experiences. (See Chapter 5.)

Knowledge: According to the traditional analysis, justified true belief; more recently, in light of the Gettier problem, epistemologists have added a fourth condition of one sort or another. (See Chapter 5.)

Logical positivism: The view of the Vienna Circle that philosophy should use modern logic (deriving from Frege and Russell), various analytical techniques, and the verification principle to restrict philosophical pursuits to the advancement of observational "scientific" knowledge, thereby banishing metaphysical concerns from philosophy. (See Chapter 6.)

Metaphysics: The philosophical study of what there is in general, including the kinds of real things; Aristotle called it the science of being *as* being.

Naive realism: The view that things really are just as they seem to be in ordinary perceptual experience.

Naturalism: The view that the natural sciences have a kind of method-ological or ontological priority in explaining how the world is; it comes in, for example, reductive, nonreductive, and eliminative forms.

Naturalized epistemology: A view of epistemology as being somehow a branch of, or at least continuous with, the natural sciences.

Necessary truth: A truth that could not have been false; the truths of logic and mathematics are paradigmatic examples of necessary truths, according to many philosophers. For example, it could not be false that if you are reading this glossary, then you are reading this glossary.

Normative: Having to do with norms, or standards of evaluation; the normative contrasts with what is merely descriptive.

Objectivity: The common feature of things whose existence does not depend on their being conceived, perceived, or believed to exist.

Ontology: The philosophical study of existence in general, e.g., of the kinds of things that exist.

Pragmatism: The view that either meaning, truth, or knowledge some-how depends on purpose-relative, practical considerations. C. S. Peirce, William James, John Dewey, and C. I. Lewis endorsed differ-ent versions of pragmatism.

Proposition: The meaningful truth-bearer expressed by a declarative sen-tence; sentences in different languages can express the same mean-ingful proposition.

Rationalism: The view that some knowledge does not depend on the evi-dence of the senses. (*Strict* rationalism: the view that no knowledge depends on the evidence of the senses, and genuine knowledge does exist.) (See Chapter 6.)

Realism: The view that some thing or class of things exists but does not depend for its existence on a conceiver's experiencing, conceiving of, or having a belief about that thing or class of things, even if the things in question are themselves mental states.

Regress problem: The difficulty of explaining the nature of inferential jus-tification, that is, one belief's being justified on the basis of another belief. (See Chapter 5.)

Relativism: With regard to truth, the view that what is true may vary among persons or among cultures, owing to differences in funda-mental beliefs or attitudes. (See Chapter 4.)

Reliabilism: The contemporary view that epistemic justification for beliefs is determined by the reliability, or truth conduciveness, of the sources of beliefs. (See Chapter 5.)

Replacement naturalism: The extreme version of naturalism implying that the natural sciences have an explanatory monopoly on all things cognitive, including cognitively significant vocabulary, claims, and disciplines. (See Chapter 2.)

Replacement pragmatism: The contemporary view that considerations of usefulness should replace traditional philosophical concerns about objective truth, or how the world really is. (See Chapter 2.)

Semantic holism: The view that the meaning of any statement depends on the meaning of some other statement(s); this is not to be confused with epistemic holism, or epistemic coherentism.

Skepticism: The epistemological view that we either cannot have or at least do not have knowledge or justified belief; this view may be restricted to a certain domain of alleged knowledge or justification, e.g., knowledge of other minds, knowledge by induction, knowledge of the past, knowledge of the objective world. (See Chapter 8.)

Synthetic truth: A statement that is true in virtue of considerations other than the meanings of the constituent terms; the truths of the sciences are paradigmatic examples of synthetic truths.

Transparency of belief: The alleged feature of beliefs making their contents immediately accessible to believers. (See Chapter 3.)

Triangulation: The activity of justifying a belief by invoking a variety of methods or sources of evidence. Many assume that beliefs arrived at by triangulation are, in general, better justified than those arrived at by a single method or from a single source. (See Chapter 6.)

Underdetermination: The claim that no set of evidence ever uniquely determines one theory decisively above all its competitors as being true; more than one theory will be possible for any set of evidence.

Verification principle: The view that the meaning of a proposition is its method of verification. This principle was endorsed by Wittgenstein in the late 1920s and by various logical positivists associated with the Vienna Circle founded by Moritz Schlick.

References

Alston, William. 1985. "Concepts of Epistemic Justification." *The Monist* 68, 57–89. Reprinted in Alston 1989, pp. 81–114.

———. 1989. *Epistemic Justification*. Ithaca, N.Y.: Cornell University Press.

Annis, David. 1978. "A Contextualist Theory of Epistemic Justification." *American Philosophical Quarterly* 15, 213–19.

Armstrong, David M. 1973. *Belief, Truth, and Knowledge*. Cambridge: Cambridge University Press.

Audi, Robert. 1993. *The Structure of Justification*. Cambridge: Cambridge University Press.

Barkow, Jerome, Cosmides, Leda, and Tooby, John, eds. 1992. *The Adapted Mind*. Oxford: Oxford University Press.

Beaumont, William. [1833] 1929, fascimile edition. *Experiments and Observations on the Gastric Juice and the Physiology of Digestion*. Cambridge, Mass.: Harvard University Press.

Berkeley, George. [1709] 1910. *An Essay Towards a New Theory of Vision*. London: Dent.

Blanshard, Brand. 1939. *The Nature of Thought*, Vol. 2. London: Allen and Unwin.

——. 1980. "Reply to Nicholas Rescher." In P.A. Schilpp, ed., *The Philosophy of Brand Blanshard*, pp. 589–600. LaSalle, Ill.: Open Court.

BonJour, Laurence. 1985. *The Structure of Empirical Knowledge*. Cambridge, Mass.: Harvard University Press.

Boyle, Robert. [1660] 1965. *New Experiments Physicomechanical Touching the Spring of the Air and its Effects*. In Boyle, *The Works*, Vol. 1. Edited by Thomas Birch. Hildesheim: Greg Olms Verlagsbuchhandlung.

Carnap, Rudolf. 1950. *The Logical Foundations of Probability*. Chicago: University of Chicago Press.

Chisholm, Roderick. 1977. *Theory of Knowledge*, 2d ed. Englewood Cliffs, N.J.: Prentice Hall.

——. 1982. *The Problem of the Criterion*. Milwaukee: Marquette University Press.

——. 1989. *The Theory of Knowledge*, 3d ed. Englewood Cliffs, N.J.: Prentice Hall.

Churchland, Paul. 1989. *A Neurocomputational Perspective*. Cambridge, Mass.: MIT Press.

Cohen, L.J. 1981. "Can Human Irrationality Be Experimentally Demonstrated?" *Behavioral and Brain Sciences* 4, 317–70.

——. 1986. *The Dialogue of Reason*. Oxford: Oxford University Press.

Cornman, James. 1975. *Perception, Common Sense, and Science*. New Haven, Conn.: Yale University Press.

——. 1980. *Skepticism, Justification, and Explanation*. Dordrecht: Kluwer.

Cosmides, Leda, and Tooby, John. 1992. "Cognitive Adaptations for Social Exchange." In J. H. Barkow, Leda Cosmides, and John Tooby, eds., *The Adapted Mind*, pp. 163–228. New York: Oxford University Press.

Davidson, Donald. 1980. *Inquiries into Truth and Interpretation*. Oxford: Oxford University Press.

Dennett, Daniel. 1987. "Three Kinds of Intentionality." In Dennett, *The Intentional Stance*. Cambridge, Mass.: MIT Press.

Descartes, René. [1640] 1991. "Letter to Mersenne, 31 December 1640." In *The Philosophical Writings of Descartes, Vol. 3: The Correspondence*, pp. 165–66. Translated by John Cottingham, Anthony Kenny, et al. Cambridge: Cambridge University Press.

Douglas, Mary. 1981. *Edward Evans-Pritchard*. New York: Penguin.

Dretske, Fred I. 1981. *Knowledge and the Flow of Information*. Cambridge, Mass.: MIT Press.

Evans-Pritchard, Edward. 1972. *Witchcraft, Oracles, and Magic among the Azande*. Oxford: Oxford University Press.

Firth, Roderick. 1969. "Lewis on the Given." In P.A. Schilpp, ed., *The Philosophy of C.I. Lewis*, pp. 329–50. LaSalle, Ill.: Open Court.

Fischoff, Baruch. 1991. "Value Elicitation: Is There Anything in There?" *American Psychologist* 46, 835–47.

Fodor, Jerry. 1975. *The Language of Thought*. Cambridge, Mass.: MIT Press.

———. 1981. *Representations*. Cambridge, Mass.: MIT Press.

———. 1983. *Modularity of Mind*. Cambridge, Mass.: MIT Press.

Foley, Richard. 1987. *The Theory of Epistemic Rationality*. Cambridge, Mass.: Harvard University Press.

Gardner, Howard. 1987. *The Mind's New Science*. New York: Basic Books.

Geertz, Clifford. 1983. *Local Knowledge*. New York: Basic Books.

Gettier, Edmund. 1963. "Is Justified True Belief Knowledge?" *Analysis* 23, 121–23.

Gigerenzer, Gerd. 1991. "How to Make Cognitive Illusions Disappear: Beyond 'Heuristics and Biases'." *European Review of Social Psychology* 2, 83–115.

Gilovich, Thomas. 1991. *How We Know What Isn't So*. New York: Free Press.

Goldman, Alan. 1988. *Empirical Knowledge*. Berkeley, Calif.: University of California Press.

Goldman, Alvin I. 1967. "A Causal Theory of Knowing." *Journal of Philosophy* 64, 357–72.

———. 1986. *Epistemology and Cognition*. Cambridge, Mass.: Harvard University Press.

———. 1992. *Liaisons: Philosophy Meets the Cognitive and Social Sciences*. Cambridge, Mass.: MIT Press.

Griggs, R.A., and Cox, J.R. 1982. "The Elusive Thematic–Materials Effect in Wason's Selection Task." *British Journal of Psychology* 73, 407–20.

Harman, Gilbert. 1986. *Change in View*. Cambridge, Mass.: MIT Press.

Helm, Paul. 1994. *Belief Policies*. Cambridge: Cambridge University Press.

Hempel, Carl. 1965. *Aspects of Scientific Explanation*. New York: Free Press.

Hess, E.H. 1975. "The Role of Pupil Size in Communication." In Rita Atkinson and Richard Atkinson, eds., *Mind and Behavior*. San Francisco: Freeman, 1980.

Hume, David. [1748] 1975. *An Enquiry Concerning Human Understanding*, edited by L.A. Selby-Bigge, 3rd ed. revised by P.H. Nidditch. Oxford: Clarendon Press.

Kitcher, Philip. 1992. "The Naturalists Return." *Philosophical Review* 101, 53–114.

Kripke, Saul. 1980. *Naming and Necessity*. Cambridge, Mass.: Harvard University Press.

Lehrer, Keith. 1990. *Theory of Knowledge*. Boulder, Col.: Westview.

Lewis, C.I. 1946. *An Analysis of Knowledge and Valuation*. LaSalle, Ill.: Open Court.

Loftus, Elizabeth and Ketcham, Katherine. 1994. *The Myth of Repressed Memory*. New York: St. Martin's Press.

Lord, C. G., Ross, Lee, and Lepper, M.R. 1979. "Biased Assimilation and Attitude Polarization: The Effects of Prior Theories on Subsequently Considered Evidence." *Journal of Personality and Social Psychology* 37, 2098–109.

Malcolm, Norman. 1942. "Moore and Ordinary Language." In P.A. Schilpp, ed., *The Philosophy of G.E. Moore*, pp. 345–68. Evanston, Ill.: Northwestern University Press.

Meyers, Robert. 1988. *The Likelihood of Knowledge*. Dordrecht: Kluwer.

Montaigne, Michel de. [1576] 1933. "Apology for Raimund Sebond." In *The Essays of Montaigne*. New York: Modern Library.

Moore, G.E. 1899. "The Nature of Judgement." *Mind*, n.s., 8, 176–93.

———. 1925. "A Defence of Common Sense." In J.H. Muirhead, ed., *Contemporary British Philosophy*, 2d Series, pp. 193–223. London: Allen and Unwin.

———. 1939. "Proof of an External World." *Proceedings of the British Academy* 25, 273–300.

———. 1941. "Certainty." In Moore, *Philosophical Papers*, pp. 227–51. London: Allen and Unwin, 1959.

Morawetz, Thomas. 1978. *Wittgenstein and Knowledge*. Amherst, Mass.: University of Massachusetts Press.

Moser, Paul K. 1989. *Knowledge and Evidence*. Cambridge: Cambridge University Press.

———. 1993. *Philosophy After Objectivity*. New York: Oxford University Press.

Nisbett, Richard, and Ross, Lee. 1980. *Human Inference: Strategies and Shortcomings*. Englewood Cliffs, N.J.: Prentice Hall.

Pap, Arthur. 1958. *Semantics and Necessary Truth*. New Haven, Conn.: Yale University Press.

Pollock, John. 1986. *Contemporary Theories of Knowledge*. Lanham, Md.: Rowman and Littlefield.

Quine, W.V. 1951. "Two Dogmas of Empiricism." In Quine, *From a Logical Point of View*, 2d ed. Cambridge, Mass.: Harvard University Press, 1961.

——— . 1954."The Language and Scope of Science." In Quine, *The Ways of Paradox*. New York: Random House, 1966.

——— . 1960. *Word and Object*. Cambridge, Mass.: MIT Press.

——— . 1969. "Epistemology Naturalized." In Quine, *Ontological Relativity and Other Essays*. New York: Columbia University Press.

——— . 1981. *Theories and Things*. Cambridge, Mass.: Harvard University Press.

——— . 1990. *Pursuit of Truth*. Cambridge, Mass.: Harvard University Press.

Rescher, Nicholas. 1979. *Cognitive Systematization*. Oxford: Blackwell.

Rorty, Richard. 1982. *Consequences of Pragmatism*. Minneapolis: University of Minnesota Press.

Russell, Bertrand. 1912. *The Problems of Philosophy*. Oxford: Oxford University Press.

——— . 1927. *Philosophy*. London: Norton.

——— . 1940. *An Inquiry into Meaning and Truth*. London: Allen and Unwin.

——— . 1944. "My Mental Development." In P.A. Schilpp, ed., *The Philosophy of Bertrand Russell*, pp. 3–20. Evanston, Ill.: Northwestern University Press.

——— . 1948. *Human Knowledge: Its Scope and Limits*. New York: Simon & Schuster.

——— . 1950. "Logical Positivism." In Russell, *Logic and Knowledge*, pp. 367–82. Edited by R.C. Marsh. London: Allen and Unwin, 1956.

——— . 1959. *My Philosophical Development*. London: Allen and Unwin.

Sellars, Wilfrid. 1975. "Epistemic Principles." In H.-N. Castañeda, ed., *Action, Knowledge, and Reality*, pp. 332–48. Indianapolis, Ind.: Bobbs-Merrill.

Sextus Empiricus. 1933. *Outlines of Pyrrhonism*. Translated by R.G. Bury. Cambridge, Mass.: Harvard University Press.

Simon, Herbert. 1983. *Reason in Human Affairs*. Stanford: Stanford University Press.

Sosa, Ernest. 1991. *Knowledge in Perspective*. Cambridge: Cambridge University Press.

Stich, Stephen. 1978. "Belief and Subdoxastic States." *Philosophy of Science* 45, 499–518.

——— . 1983. *From Folk Psychology to Cognitive Science: The Case Against Belief*. Cambridge, Mass.: MIT Press.

——— . 1990. "Rationality." In Daniel Osherson and Edward Smith, eds., *Thinking: An Invitation to Cognitive Science*, Vol. 3, pp. 173–96. Cambridge, Mass.: MIT Press.

Stroud, Barry. 1984. *The Significance of Philosophical Scepticism.* Oxford: Oxford University Press.

Taylor, Charles. 1982. "Rationality." In Martin Hollis and Steven Lukes, eds., *Rationality and Relativism*, pp. 87–105. Oxford: Blackwell.

Trout, J.D. 1998. *Measuring the Intentional World.* New York: Oxford Unversity Press.

Tversky, Amos, and Kahneman, Daniel. 1973. "Availability: A Heuristic for Judging Frequency and Probability." *Cognitive Psychology* 5, 207–32.

—— . 1974. "Judgment under Uncertainty: Heuristics and Biases." *Science* 185, 1124–31.

—— . 1986. "Rational Choice and the Framing of Decisions." In K. S. Cook and M. Levi, eds., *The Limits of Rationality*, pp. 60–89. Chicago: University of Chicago Press.

Wason, Peter, and Johnson-Laird, Philip. 1972. *Psychology of Reasoning.* Cambridge, Mass.: Harvard University Press.

Winch, Peter. 1964. "Understanding a Primitive Society." *American Philosophical Quarterly* 1, 307–24. Reprinted in B.R. Wilson, ed., *Rationality*, pp. 78–111. New York: Harper and Row, 1970.

Wittgenstein, Ludwig. 1958. *Philosophical Investigations*, 3d ed. Translated by G.E.M. Anscombe. London: Macmillan.

—— . 1969. *On Certainty.* Oxford: Blackwell.

Further Reading

1. Epistemology: A First Look

ANTHOLOGIES

Dancy, Jonathan, and Sosa, Ernest, eds. 1992. *A Companion to Epistemology*. Oxford: Blackwell. (This is a reference work with brief articles on many topics in epistemology, including a short bibliography for each topic.)

French, P.A., Uehling, T.E., and Wettstein, H.K., eds. 1980. *Midwest Studies in Philosophy, Vol. V: Studies in Epistemology*. Minneapolis: University of Minnesota Press.

Moser, Paul K., and vander Nat, Arnold, eds. 1995. *Human Knowledge: Classical and Contemporary Approaches*, 2d ed. New York: Oxford University Press.

Nagel, Ernest, and Brandt, Richard, eds. 1965. *Meaning and Knowledge: Systematic Readings in Epistemology*. New York: Harcourt, Brace, and World.

AUTHORED WORKS

Chisholm, Roderick M. 1989. *Theory of Knowledge*, 3d ed. Englewood Cliffs, N.J.: Prentice Hall.

Hill, Thomas. 1961. *Contemporary Theories of Knowledge.* New York: Macmillan.

Lehrer, Keith. 1990. *Theory of Knowledge.* Boulder, Col.: Westview.

Russell, Bertrand. 1912. *The Problems of Philosophy.* Oxford: Oxford University Press.

2. Explaining Knowledge

ANTHOLOGIES

Goldman, Alvin I., ed. 1993. *Readings in Philosophy and Cognitive Science.* Cambridge, Mass.: MIT Press.

Kornblith, Hilary, ed. 1994. *Naturalizing Epistemology,* 2d ed. Cambridge, Mass.: MIT Press.

Tomberlin, J.E., ed. 1988. *Philosophical Perspectives, Vol. 2: Epistemology.* Atascadero, Calif.: Ridgeview.

AUTHORED WORKS

Goldman, Alvin I. 1986. *Epistemology and Cognition.* Cambridge, Mass.: Harvard University Press.

Pollock, John. 1986. *Contemporary Theories of Knowledge.* Lanham, Md.: Rowman and Littlefield.

Quine, W.V. 1990. *Pursuit of Truth.* Cambridge, Mass.: Harvard University Press.

Sosa, Ernest. 1991. *Knowledge in Perspective.* Cambridge: Cambridge University Press.

3. Belief

ANTHOLOGIES

Bogdan, R.J., ed. 1986. *Belief: Form, Content, and Function.* Oxford: Oxford University Press.

Cassam, Quassim, ed. 1994. *Self-Knowledge.* Oxford: Oxford University Press.

Greenwood, John D., ed. 1991. *The Future of Folk Psychology.* Cambridge: Cambridge University Press.

Griffiths, A.P., ed. 1967. *Knowledge and Belief.* Oxford: Oxford University Press.

Salmon, Nathan, and Soames, Scott, eds. 1988. *Propositions and Attitudes.* Oxford: Oxford University Press.

AUTHORED WORKS

Baker, Lynn Rudder. 1987. *Saving Belief.* Princeton: Princeton University Press.

Cohen, L.J. 1992. *An Essay on Belief and Acceptance.* Oxford: Oxford University Press.

Fodor, Jerry. 1987. *Psychosemantics: The Problem of Meaning in the Philosophy of Mind.* Cambridge, Mass.: MIT Press.

Garfield, Jay L. 1988. *Belief in Psychology: A Study in the Ontology of Mind.* Cambridge, Mass.: MIT Press.

Stich, Stephen. 1983. *From Folk Psychology to Cognitive Science: The Case Against Belief.* Cambridge, Mass.: MIT Press.

4. Truth

ANTHOLOGIES

Harris, James F., and Severens, Richard H., eds. 1970. *Analyticity: Selected Readings.* Chicago: Quadrangle.

Moore, A.W., ed. 1993. *Meaning and Reference.* Oxford: Oxford University Press.

Pitcher, George, ed. 1964. *Truth.* Englewood Cliffs, N.J.: PrenticeHall.

AUTHORED WORKS

Alston, William P. 1996. *A Realist Conception of Truth.* Ithaca, N.Y.: Cornell University Press.

Davidson, Donald. 1984. *Inquiries into Truth and Interpretation.* Oxford: Oxford University Press.

Devitt, Michael. 1991. *Realism and Truth,* 2d ed. Oxford: Blackwell.

Kirkham, Richard L. 1992. *Theories of Truth.* Cambridge, Mass.: MIT Press.

Mackie, J.L. 1973. *Truth, Probability, and Paradox.* Oxford: Oxford University Press.

5. Justification and Beyond

ANTHOLOGIES

Bender, John W., ed. 1989. *The Current State of the Coherence Theory.* Dordrecht: Kluwer.

Moser, Paul K., ed. 1996. *Empirical Knowledge*, 2d ed. Lanham, Md.: Rowman and Littlefield.

Pappas, George S., ed. 1979. *Justification and Knowledge*. Dordrecht: D. Reidel.

Pappas, George S., and Swain, Marshall, eds. 1978. *Essays on Knowledge and Justification*. Ithaca, N.Y.: Cornell University Press.

AUTHORED WORKS

Alston, William P. 1989. *Epistemic Justification*. Ithaca, N.Y.: Cornell University Press.

Audi, Robert. 1993. *The Structure of Justification*. Cambridge: Cambridge University Press.

BonJour, Laurence. 1985. *The Structure of Empirical Knowledge*. Cambridge, Mass.: Harvard University Press.

Chisholm, Roderick M. 1982. *The Foundations of Knowing*. Minneapolis: University of Minnesota Press.

Foley, Richard. 1987. *The Theory of Epistemic Rationality*. Cambridge, Mass.: Harvard University Press.

Goldman, Alvin I. 1992. *Liaisons: Philosophy Meets the Cognitive and Social Sciences*. Cambridge, Mass.: MIT Press.

Moser, Paul K. 1989. *Knowledge and Evidence*. Cambridge: Cambridge University Press.

Sosa, Ernest. 1991. *Knowledge in Perspective*. Cambridge: Cambridge University Press.

6. Sources of Knowledge

ANTHOLOGIES

Akins, Kathleen, ed. 1995. *Perception*. New York: Oxford University Press.

Antony, Louise, and Witt, Charlotte, eds. 1993. *A Mind of One's Own*. Boulder, Col.: Westview.

Dancy, Jonathan, ed. 1988. *Perceptual Knowledge*. Oxford: Oxford University Press.

Schmitt, Frederick F., ed. 1994. *Socializing Epistemology: The Social Dimensions of Knowledge*. Lanham, Md.: Rowman and Littlefield.

Sperber, Dan, Premack, David, and Premack, Ann, eds. 1995. *Causal Cognition: A Multidisciplinary Debate*. Oxford: Oxford University Press.

Stich, Stephen, ed.. 1975. *Innate Ideas*. Berkeley: University of California Press.

AUTHORED WORKS

Carruthers, Peter. 1992. *Human Knowledge and Human Nature*. Oxford: Oxford University Press.

Coady, C.A.J. 1992. *Testimony: A Philosophical Study*. Oxford: Oxford University Press.

Coffa, J. Alberto. 1991. *The Semantic Tradition from Kant to Carnap: To the Vienna Station*. Cambridge: Cambridge University Press.

Cornman, James. 1975. *Perception, Common Sense, and Science*. New Haven, Conn.: Yale University Press.

Dretske, Fred I. 1981. *Knowledge and the Flow of Information*. Cambridge, Mass.: MIT Press.

Elman, Jeffrey L., Bates, Elizabeth A., Johnson, Mark H., et al. 1996. *Rethinking Innateness*. Cambridge, Mass.: MIT Press.

Gardner, Howard. 1987. *The Mind's New Science: A History of the Cognitive Revolution*. New York: Basic Books.

Goldman, Alvin I. 1986. *Epistemology and Cognition*. Cambridge, Mass.: Harvard University Press.

7. Rationality

ANTHOLOGIES

Benn, S.I. and Mortimore, G.W., eds. 1976. *Rationality and the Social Sciences*. London: Routledge.

Cook, Karen S. and Levi, Margaret, eds. 1990. *The Limits of Rationality*. Chicago: University of Chicago Press.

Elster, Jon, ed. 1986. *Rational Choice*. New York: New York University Press.

Hollis, Martin, and Lukes, Steven, eds. 1982. *Rationality and Relativism*. Oxford: Blackwell.

Kahneman, Daniel, Slovic, Paul, and Tversky, Amos, eds. 1982. *Judgment under Uncertainty: Heuristics and Biases*. Cambridge: Cambridge University Press.

Moser, Paul K., ed. 1990. *Rationality in Action*. Cambridge: Cambridge University Press.

Wilson, Bryan R., ed. 1970. *Rationality*. New York: Harper and Row.

AUTHORED WORKS

Dawes, Robyn M. 1988. *Rational Choice in an Uncertain World*. New York: Harcourt, Brace, Jovanovich.

Foley, Richard. 1993. *Working Without a Net*. New York: Oxford University Press.

Gilovich, Thomas. 1991. *How We Know What Isn't So.* New York: Free Press.

Rescher, Nicholas. 1988. *Rationality.* Oxford: Oxford University Press.

Simon, Herbert. 1983. *Reason in Human Affairs.* Stanford: Stanford University Press.

Stein, Edward. 1996. *Without Good Reason: The Rationality Debate in Philosophy and Cognitive Science.* Oxford: Oxford University Press.

Stich, Stephen. 1990. *The Fragmentation of Reason.* Cambridge, Mass.: MIT Press.

8. Skepticism

ANTHOLOGIES

Burnyeat, Myles, ed. 1983. *The Skeptical Tradition.* Berkeley: University of California Press.

Clay, Marjorie, and Lehrer, Keith, eds. 1989. *Knowledge and Skepticism.* Boulder, Col.: Westview.

Luper-Foy, Steven, ed. 1987. *The Possibility of Knowledge.* Lanham, Md.: Rowman and Littlefield.

Roth, Michael, and Ross, Glenn, eds. 1990. *Doubting: Contemporary Perspectives on Skepticism.* Dordrecht: Kluwer.

AUTHORED WORKS

Alston, William P. 1993. *The Reliability of Sense Perception.* Ithaca, N.Y.: Cornell University Press.

Amico, Robert P. 1993. *The Problem of the Criterion.* Lanham, Md.: Rowman and Littlefield.

Fogelin, Robert J. 1994. *Pyrrhonian Reflections on Knowledge and Justification.* New York: Oxford University Press.

Fumerton, Richard. 1995. *Metaepistemology and Skepticism.* Lanham, Md.: Rowman and Littlefield.

Moser, Paul K. 1993. *Philosophy After Objectivity.* New York: Oxford University Press.

Rescher, Nicholas. 1980. *Scepticism.* Oxford: Blackwell.

Strawson, P.F. 1985. *Skepticism and Naturalism: Some Varieties.* New York: Columbia University Press.

Stroud, Barry. 1984. *The Significance of Philosophical Scepticism.* Oxford: Oxford University Press.

9. Epistemology and Explanation

ANTHOLOGIES

Boyd, R., Gasper, P., and Trout, J.D., eds. 1991. *The Philosophy of Science.* Cambridge, Mass.: MIT Press/Bradford Books.

Knowles, Dudley, ed. 1990. *Explanation and Its Limits.* Cambridge: Cambridge University Press.

Ruben, David-Hillel, ed. 1993. *Explanation.* Oxford: Oxford University Press.

THORED WORKS

nkel, Alan. 1981. *Forms of Explanation.* New Haven, Conn.: Yale University Press.

n, Alan H. 1988. *Empirical Knowledge.* Berkeley: University of California Press.

ilbert. 1973. *Thought.* Princeton: Princeton University Press.

rl G. 1965. *Aspects of Scientific Explanation.* New York: Free

1993. *The Advancement of Science.* New York: Oxford Uni-

)1. *Inference to the Best Explanation.* London: Routledge.

1988. *Judgement and Justification.* Cambridge: Cambridge Press.

. *Four Decades of Scientific Explanation.* Minneapolis: sota Press.

Computational Philosophy of Science. Cambridge,

ϱ the Intentional World. New York: Oxford Uni-

Index